In Tongues of
Mortals and Angels

In Tongues of
Mortals and Angels

A Deconstructive Theology of
God-Talk in Acts and Corinthians

Eric D. Barreto
Jacob D. Myers
Thelathia "Nikki" Young

LEXINGTON BOOKS/FORTRESS ACADEMIC
Lanham • Boulder • New York • London

Published by Lexington Books/Fortress Academic

Lexington Books is an imprint of The Rowman & Littlefield Publishing Group, Inc.
4501 Forbes Boulevard, Suite 200, Lanham, Maryland 20706
www.rowman.com

6 Tinworth Street, London SE11 5AL, United Kingdom

British Library Cataloguing in Publication Information Available

Library of Congress Cataloging-in-Publication Data

Names: Barreto, Eric D., 1980– author.
Title: In tongues of mortals and angels : a deconstructive theology of God-talk in
    Acts and Corinthians / Eric D. Barreto, Jacob D. Myers, Thelathia "Nikki" Young.
Description: Lanham, MD : Fortress Academic, 2018. | Includes bibliographical
    references and index.
Identifiers: LCCN 2018045973 (print) | LCCN 2018047867 (ebook) | ISBN
    9781978706828 (electronic) | ISBN 9781978706811 (cloth : alk. paper)
Subjects: LCSH: Bible. Acts—Criticism, interpretation, etc. | Bible. Corinthians,
    1st—Criticism, interpretation, etc. | Speech acts (Linguistics)—Religious
    aspects—Christianity.
Classification: LCC BS2625.52 (ebook) | LCC BS2625.52 .B373 2018 (print) |
    DDC 226/.06—dc23
LC record available at https://lccn.loc.gov/2018045973

∞™ The paper used in this publication meets the minimum requirements of American National Standard for Information Sciences—Permanence of Paper for Printed Library Materials, ANSI/NISO Z39.48-1992.

Printed in the United States of America

Jacob, Nikki, and Eric dedicate this book to our teachers, respectively:

To Ron Williams,
for "stirring up the gift of God that is within me" (2 Tim. 1:6–7)

To Mary E. Mckay, my aunt,
for showing me what it means and what it takes to SHOUT

To Richard Luckert,
for teaching me the inimitable power of my
voice alongside the voices of others

Contents

Introduction

The underlying conviction of the three authors of this book is that we can speak about God today. We confess that God empowers speech in the church, academy, and world. We dare to hope that we might speak not just *about* God but *with* God.

Church history is replete with examples of speech that is about God and that is empowered by God. God has revealed Godself to be in the business of calling all people to bear witness to God's work in the world. Without minimizing these instantiations of divine discourse through the tongues of mortals, the three of us hope to lend biblical, theological, and ethical support to God-talk today.

Speaking of God in our current sociopolitical contexts is fraught. Much contemporary God-talk is either vacuous or abusive, tending to reduce divine discourse to bromides or facile fundamentalisms on the one hand or to ignore or erase the material realities of our speech under the banner of neoliberalism. That is, our argument is not that there is a lack of God-talk in our midst; it's that such God-talk is not true to the liberative and transformative edge of the gospel. Too often, Scripture and its God-talk are treated as either the entirety of revelation or as an inert companion in tackling the world's problems. We speak against such contemporary bifurcations of Scripture by attending to the phenomenon of divine discourse in Scripture and highlighting the importance of such speech for academic, ecclesial, and sociopolitical discourse.

Through close textual engagement, theological exposition, and ethical reflection, we present a (de)constructive theology of divine speech in the Acts of the Apostles and the Letters of Paul in critical conversation with contemporary issues of sociopolitical, ecclesial, and theological importance. In particular, we attend to texts in Acts and 1 Corinthians that open up fresh ways of thinking about divine discourse, preaching, and agency in light of emerging matters of theological and ethical import. In addition to classical modes of textual and theological analysis, we turn to the sociopolitical and sociolinguistic aspects of speech as they become manifest in these pericopes. As such, we are simultaneously deconstructing these texts through postcolonial, poststructural, and queer frames of analysis, embracing an alterity that each reveals in its own way, an alterity that has been muted too often by biblical interpretation and theological work.

WHY ATTEND TO SCRIPTURE TOGETHER?

We forward that Scripture remains a fecund site for revelation, a theological space wherein human flourishing can be imagined anew. More than an ancient mythology or a modern rulebook, Scripture is a source of renewed imagination about how God and God's servants might speak today. Our focus on Acts and 1 Corinthians is at the center of this endeavor; it is not an incidental selection. In both these biblical texts, we find a preponderance of language around the Spirit and the way the Spirit imbues humans with the ability to speak.

In addition, we have two biblical books that have suffered problematic interpretation. Many have read Acts as a guide for an ideal church, a blueprint for how to build such an ecclesiology. Such a reading misses how the protagonists of Acts are empowered by God to narrate the church at its best *and* its worst. 1 Corinthians has drawn attention due to its references to ecstatic speech, but we wish to help our readers imagine God-talk as ordinary and rooted in human communities and concerns. In this way, ecstatic speech can stand in creative tension with quotidian forms of God-talk. Additionally, readers often note the flaws of the Corinthian church, finding here a negative example for congregational life. That is, the church in Acts stands as a model church and in 1 Corinthians as a cautionary tale. Such a distinction misreads both texts.

Our aim, therefore, is to help scholars and graduate students heading into church, parachurch, and/or academic vocations to reclaim a mode of speaking *about* and *with* God that is empowered by the Holy Spirit. Especially for mainline and evangelical Christians, who tend to ignore the ecstatic manifestation of the Holy Spirit through tongue-speaking, we offer an alternative hermeneutic that views speaking in tongues as modes of speech that disrupt and disturb the socio-linguistic foundations of so-called rational discourses. We want to lead our readers to speak boldly to the powers and principalities through speech oriented to justice and through deconstructive speech that undermines the a priori philosophical commitments of language in the church, academy, and world.

In short, our talk *about* and *with* God is theological precisely when such speech undercuts the prevailing colonial, imperial, and oppressive discourses that inform and shape our lives and when such speech declares and embodies the good news that we are free from such oppression. Such speech will empower and catalyze new modes of theological and ethical engagement with contemporary issues besetting both the church and society. Such speech is most theological in its attention to deeply human concerns.

Moreover, we seek to model an interdisciplinary approach to theological discourse that is simultaneously infused with biblical interrogations and ethical motivations. We recognize that there are different modes of understanding God-talk, and so we invite readers into a rich, complex, and robust engagement with theological questions that draws on their own complicated, multi-focused, plurally derived interests. We aim to confront and transcend the silos from which biblical, theological, and ethical discourses normally emerge and open the dialogue among scholars and students in a dialogically generative way. Our respective guilds contribute vocabularies and semantic structures that bolster certain modes of discourse while muting others. But this is no excuse. We are called to speak from our particular cultures to overlapping yet disparate cultures. We need to find those points of convergence and divergence across disciplines because we only hear ourselves—and in distorted ways—when we speak in echo chambers.

HOW DID WE ATTEND TO SCRIPTURE TOGETHER?

In this book, form follows and facilitates function. We have written and organized the text in a way that moves us beyond the bounds of disciplinary conventions and the methods of argumentation. Those machinations and the implications they bear are not the aim of this book.

Instead, this book marks an exploration. It is less a product of our work than a working project. We aim to model a way of approaching biblical texts differently than the ways in which we have been trained. It was a new experience for us to begin a project without knowing for sure where we would end up. Even as we were haunted throughout with questions of efficacy, about whether or not this would *work*, we pressed forward in the hope that our collective and reflective engagement would yield something other than what we could have expected.

Several questions guided our work together: What might it mean for communities to value experimentation over expertise? What would it mean for us to care more about process than content? How might such an orientation to God, the world, and community transform us? How might the Spirit reframe us in the doing and in the being together? What forms of speech and patterns of belonging might be inaugurated in us through this process?

These are not the kinds of questions we were trained to ask, much less answer. But having abided together with these texts and having listened to and learned from one another, we are prepared to offer some preliminary responses, responses that we hope will guide you through this book.

Expertise in any endeavor is impossible to discount. Whether we're talking about bike riding, quantum computing, or biblical exegesis, once you know how to do something you can't *unknow* it. Nor should you. At the same time, even as academic and ecclesial training help us to understand biblical texts more fully, such skills can also prevent us from receiving fresh insights. It's no wonder that many significant breakthroughs in science and the arts emerge from folks without formal training or by those who are just getting started in their careers (take Einstein, for example). We learn to think in certain ways, and those ways of thinking can come to determine how we must think.

The joy of experimentation with others is that our intellectual scaffolding gets exposed. It is only when we are prompted to account for why we understand a text as we do or how we arrived at a given interpretation that we are enabled to interrogate our learned assumptions. Such experimentation requires both trust and a willingness to have your methods of biblical interpretation challenged. The book in your hands marks this kind of experimentation.

Biblical scholars have tended to focus on content. "What does this text mean?" they ask. Of course, every content presupposes a process. The latter makes the former possible. Relatively recently, we have seen biblical scholars investigate anew and with renewed vigor how our particular processes of exegesis shape biblical content. In other words, *how* texts mean structures *what* they mean.

The process of interpreting scripture in a community of difference offered us just as much (if not more) as the interpretations each of us produced individually. This by no means suggests that we entered some state of corporate bliss, a hermeneutical utopia where the veil of theological knowing was miraculously pulled back, and we were able to see God face-to-face. We did not always agree. At times, we were shocked by each other's interpretation. But in committing to the process of open and honest engagement with one another's insights, we were able to glimpse things in and through the biblical witness that would have been impossible on our own.

OUR VOICES AND THE POLITICS OF CITATION

One of the benefits of writing this book together is that we have the opportunity to experience a polyphony of thoughts, ideas, questions, and hopes that emerge from our engagements with various texts and one another. For me (Nikki), it is an experience that catches the simultaneity of visibility and erasure, heightened volumes and silence, movement and stillness, commitment and exploration, proclamation and reception. We three get to make our way through our own geography of liminality wherein the voices and ideas that we engage—including our own—are valuable because they are disparate and connected, independent and interdependent.

Yet, such an opportunity comes with the need to attend to and perhaps interrogate what voices we feature and which ones we lay aside. Even more, the same opportunity entangles itself with our individual and collective needs to navigate (both colluding with and resisting) processes of self-validation and justification within our respective fields and in the study of religion. In this book, as we attempt to manage the harmonies of our voices, engage in talk about and with God, and invoke the theories and philosophies of others in our fields, we do so knowing that our efforts are linked with and refracted through practices of naming, signifying, and validating. Thus, those efforts are also bound up with the histories and ongoing effects of colonization, intellectual imperialism, and knowledge production, as well as the academic industrial complex.

Citation practices reflect genealogies of knowledge production. We engage portions of the biblical text in this book with the understanding that our engagement reflects our interest in participating in and challenging the ways that people approach the canon of material that shapes theological perspectives, beliefs, and action. These canons house the basis for what is allowable God-talk and even form the parameters around moral imaginaries that can come from that God-talk. But we know that canons and the way that we approach them exist beyond the lines of theological projection; we know that they live in the world of power relations and knowledge formation. In fact, canons illustrate the connection between knowledge and power. Acclaimed novelist, essayist, and literary critic Toni Morrison reflects this beautifully:

> Canon building is empire building. Canon defense is national defense. Canon debate, whatever the terrain, nature, and range (of criticism, of history, of the history of knowledge, of the definition of language, the universality of aesthetic principles, the sociology of art, the humanistic imagination), is the clash of cultures. And all of the interests are vested.[1]

In this lecture, "Unspeakable Things Unspoken: The Afro-American Presence in American Literature," Morrison details the ways that naming and describing the American experience through that of the "whitemale" actually formulates the structure for understanding America. It happens on the backs and brows of black and brown people, women, children, and poor folks whose labor feeds the racist, patriarchal cycle of recognition and inheritance. The power-infused production of knowledge, as she describes it, requires but does not recognize the ongoing erasure of some experiences for the sake of exalting others.

This book puts on display our complex (and likely inadequate) attempts to write in a space of transgression, balancing the geographies of epistemic interdependence that necessarily emerge from sites of colonization, intellectual imperialism, and more while also noting that the balance itself is a practice of collusion. We expose ourselves to practices of academic aggrandizement while doing our best to let our voices shine through the material. We do this because we want to explore the ways that new perspectives, shifts in thought, and challenges to longstanding theories impact theological inquiry and possibility.

Our process, then, calls for intentional and ethical citation politics and practices. In her 2013 blogpost titled "Making Feminist Points," Sara Ahmed names citation practices as reproductive technologies that act as "a way of reproducing the world around certain bodies."[2] She suggests that the structures of citation form and shape disciplines and reflect "techniques of selection, ways of making certain bodies and thematics core to the discipline, and others not even a part."[3] She's not wrong. More often than not, academics cite others who are already famous, even when those people are using ideas from unknown, up-and-coming, under-resourced, and minoritized folks who have created and produced knowledge and information.

Thus, the politics and ethical practices of citation call us three to contend with what it means for minoritized people to have voice, to *be*. One of our major hopes is to bring into our work voices that have been overlooked, undervalued, and hypercriticized, without marking them as peripheral. This includes bringing our own voices to bear on conversations and ideas to which we may not have previously had access. Even more, it means featuring thinkers whose ideas propel our talk about God in directions and areas that we had not considered and that stretch us in ways that strengthen our connections with others.

In this book, sometimes we get it right, and sometimes readers will notice that we are simply trying to figure out the balance between exposure and exploitation, between acknowledgment and appropriation. We want to know our limits while not being limited by what we know. It is tricky business, really, and we invite you to join us in the work of navigating the terrains of complexity that stretch out before us.

PLAN OF THE BOOK

In the chapters that follow, each of us focuses on a text from Acts or 1 Corinthians that helps unfold various dimensions of what it means to speak about and with God today. At the close of each chapter, we have recorded conversations we had with one another about these chapters. These conversations are invitations into the complex imaginations towards which we point. That is, we imagine each of these chapters as invitations into further reflection and conversation less than conclusive assertions about these biblical texts.

First, in "Spirit Speech," Eric D. Barreto reads Pentecost in Acts 2 as a story that affirms and celebrates the multi-cultural, multi-ethnic, multi-lingual shape of theological reflection. Theology is not the property of a single cultural location but is most vibrant in the encounter of diverse perspectives and modes of life. Difference is, therefore, not an obstacle in God-talk; difference is theology's life blood.

In the next chapter, Jacob D. Myers examines "Bold Speech" in Acts 4. There, he reflects on the use and abuse of power and the ways that Peter's bold speech disrupts and subverts by pointing to the resurrection of Jesus and the dead along with him. The playfulness and pluriformity of Peter's language is a site rife for considering how we might speak truth to power today, even and especially when we are caught up in the discourses of the powerful.

Thelathia "Nikki" Young considers the shape of "Prophetic Speech" in Peter's recognition in Acts 10 of God's embrace of Cornelius, his household, and his friends. As she contends, "Through Peter, Luke has as much to say about the *persons* who constitute the church as it does about the value of equality *within* the church that underwrites human relations. But what the text does NOT do is erase particularity in the service of supporting this notion of nonpartiality."

Barreto turns to Paul's famous proclamation at the Areopagus in Athens to imagine "Strange Speech." Too often assumed to be a universal word because of its setting at this philosophical center, Paul's speech is actually particular to the Athens Luke imagines. Instead of a word applicable in all places and times, these words are tuned to an Athens that has lost its way. In this way, Luke continues a pattern of planting the good news in the culturally particular soil of the various places his protagonists visit.

Myers's "Baptismal Speech" explores the shape of language and discourse and the ways baptism in Jesus allows us to both draw upon and critique the structures of language we inherit. In a reading of Apollos's eloquence and his instruction by Priscilla and Aquila alongside Paul's puzzling encounter with disciples who had experienced John's baptism but not baptism in the name of Jesus, Myers concludes, "Baptismal speech presages an alternative mode of thinking, speaking, and being in the world. Such confessional stances do not merely capitulate to dominant structures of thought, speech, and action. By entering into the waters of baptism in the name of Jesus, one dies to the systems and structures that previously governed the person's thought, speech, and action."

The two next chapters turn to 1 Corinthians, first Myers on the language of mystery 2:1–16 and "Wise Speech" and Young on chapter 13's famous and potent appeal to love in "Loving Speech." Myers begins by contending, "God's power, like God's wisdom, shares no part in the logics and measures of this world. Paul does not speak of empirical verifiability; he speaks of that which is ever beyond sight and sound. He does not speak of human wisdom— of political, economic, and religious power; he speaks of the power of God, which is beyond all possibility. He does not speak of knowledge; he speaks of crucifixion." Young concludes, "It is the face-to-face experience that Paul promises. Such a lens does not allow us to ignore, erase, or marginalize one another; nor does it promote harm or dehumanization. Paul's plea for a face-to-face love is an investment in a social ethic that, were we to heed it, would insure our collective survival in the end and, more importantly, right now."

IMPLICATIONS

We are writing this book in the shadow of a long litany of moments of racial tension in the United States, moments that have shaped the three of us as teachers and scholars and activists and thinkers and people. The unrest following the shooting of Michael Brown in Ferguson, Missouri, sparked something. In Charleston, South Carolina, a worshipping community was ruptured. In Orlando, Florida, a celebration was turned into mourning. In Hempstead, Texas, an encounter with police resulted in Sandra Bland's death. Not to speak of the threat of climate change, the consistent rejection and killing of transpersons, the fear that surrounded Syrian refugees, the so-called Muslim ban, the uncertainty Dreamers face. We are writing this preface the very week after white supremacists marched on Charlottesville, Virginia. We are writing this preface the week after a white supremacist drove a car through a crowd of protesters. We are writing this preface the week after a sitting president equivocated about the nature, ferocity, and danger of white supremacy.

In other words, these concerns are not abstract for us. We feel them in our bones. They shape our sense of vocation. They shape how and why we teach, how and why we write, how and why we protest and resist. In short, these events have driven us to ask how we deploy Spirit speech in a way that challenges injustice and affirms the fullness of life Jesus inaugurated through his life and ministry.

We wonder together why we are sitting at a table writing instead of lifting signs and voices of protest on the front lines. We conclude that the intellectual and theological work we are doing provides necessary support and structure for those signs and voices of protest. Our words are not just ethereal messages we cast into the world; our words, your words, can be transformative. As Maya Angelou teaches us, "words are things." Our words, imbued by the Spirit and suffused with God's presence, can make a difference in a world gone astray.

The church, the academy, the culture at large have trained us to guard against the risk of misspeaking or being challenged. That kind of fear keeps people divided—segregated—and locks us into a limited mode of discourse. What we are doing in our writing and thinking together is bearing witness to a mystery that we have seen and heard in our engagement.

We, in our engagement with these biblical texts and with one another, have discerned whispers of angelic speech in the midst of our mortal words. But the way to move forward is to take these words as mortal words. If scholars and students will lean into their identities in search of genuine community, they just might hear the speech of angels.

NOTES

1. Toni Morrison, "Unspeakable Things Unspoken: The Afro-American Presence in American Literature," in *The Tanner Lectures on Human Values* (University of Utah Press, 1988).

2. Sara Ahmed, "Making Feminist Points," feministkilljoys (blog), September 11, 2013, https://feministkilljoys.com/2013/09/11/making-feminist-points/.

3. Ibid.

Chapter One

Spirit Speech: Acts 2:1–36

Eric D. Barreto

God speaks many languages. This might strike the preacher and the theologian as obvious. After all, God is not restrained to any one culture, any one set of words, any one language. God is the God of all creation. God can be worshipped in any language or no language whatsoever. God can be encountered in the words of worship and song as well as the silence of contemplation. Of course, God speaks many languages, for God's children speak many languages, too.

And yet, our reading of Scripture and our practices of hospitality and welcome belie this seemingly obvious conclusion. We may say we believe that God speaks many languages, but we appear not to do so. We may say we understand the limits of language and the ways in which our theologies are set in a particular cultural context. We may say that our knowledge of God is as much confession as it is apophatic mystery. Yet our preaching practices and our theological imaginations tend to imagine a monolingual God who speaks the same words we do. We tend to imagine a monocultural God who adapts the gospel to the particularities of others but not to ours. The language of the dominant culture is imagined to be an exclusive conduit for the truth of the good news. And our cultures become the media through which a pure, undistilled good news can be proclaimed.

Think, for instance, of the biblical literalism that reigns in so many American churches, a biblical literalism that rests not on the ancient languages in which these texts were composed but English translations. Churches in which the King James Version is seen as the one and only site of divine revelation are an obvious example of such a theological assumption, but they are not alone. The extremes of such a theological conception of Scripture are not isolated to a handful of churches; it worms its way into wider cultural assumptions about how Scriptures speak and teach and shape a community. In many evangelical churches, the English text is treated as infallible, inerrant. And even in mainline churches, this bibliolatry finds rich soil in various reading practices that continue to center a particular set of experiences and identities as normative. At the same time, deviations from these norms are assumed to be alternatives to reading Scripture but not as "biblical" as normed forms of reading.

In short, for too many of us, our very understanding of how God speaks is truncated by a monolingual, monocultural assumption. We expect God to speak my language and translate that message to others as needed. But *my* God speaks to *me* in the language of *my* heart. This is true in one way, a problematic approach in so many others.

Yet our assumptions about Scripture are not the only example of a theological slippage between what we say about God's ability to speak many languages and practices that betray our far more naive assumptions. In our welcoming of the stranger, we again find ourselves re-narrating and misshaping how God welcomes the so-called "other." In too many churches, hospitality is not a practice of mutual welcome; instead, we construe hospitality unilaterally. *We* welcome the refugee and the stranger. *We* welcome the marginalized. *We* welcome the so-called "other." Moreover, such hospitality is an invitation to acculturation not transformation. We invite "all" to come into *our* spaces and become like *us*. That is, those of us in dominant cultures remain the hosts of such hospitality, rarely its recipients. In framing this binary, we have already created a boundary, an "us" and a "them." That chasm, we imagine, can only be bridged by our gracious invitation. Such hospitality is safe. Such hospitality demands everything from those being hosted, very little from the host save the niceties and formalities of graciousness and politeness. Such hospitality lacks the radical edge of a God who welcomes every stranger and calls her "beloved child."[1]

The problem is not just a misshaped theology, however; the problem is that such a misshaped and misshaping theology teaches us how to be human. If we're honest, a monolingual, monocultural expectation of God too easily becomes normative and definitive. Such theology too easily dictates how we encounter our neighbor: not with love so much as tolerance, not with welcome so much as the cultural niceties we all expect. Such theology shapes how we imagine others. Such hospitality barely resembles the tables Jesus shares with sinners in the Gospels. Such hospitality is barely worthy of its name.

What we need, therefore, is a God who shatters the monolingual and monocultural enclaves within which we have restrained God's activity in this world. To do so, Scripture is most helpful. In this case, I want to turn to a text too often misread, a text whose misreading has misshapen how we imagine our differences. In the Pentecost scene in Acts 2, we encounter a

God who revels in our differences, who treasures our differences, who was the very creator of our differences. Yet we have tended to read this narrative as a moment of healing wherein our differences are obviated, our otherness wiped clean, our many languages collapsed as we retreat to a moment before the terrible curse of the Tower of Babel. In short, we have assumed that Pentecost is a reversal of Babel, that Pentecost heals our differences by bridging our linguistic differences.

This is not so.

Think for a moment about the implications of such a reading of Pentecost. After all, is it a curse that I grew up speaking Spanish? Is it a curse that the world teems with different languages? Is it not a great tragedy when the last speaker of an indigenous language passes from this earth, leaving us bereft of the rich cultural vision such a language funded? After all, when a language dies, we are not just bereft of its words but the cultural world it held and shaped and contained.[2] But if Babel is a curse, we should celebrate the death of a language and demand linguistic adherence to only one language. In fact, these are the instincts of empire: to mute differences for the sake of a dominant culture. In contrast to such imperial logics, our many languages are not a curse and yet we have read and taught Babel as a moment of divine fury meant to afflict us with many different languages. And in light of such exegetical assumptions, we have reached the narrative of Pentecost and seen there a healing of these divisive wounds.

The imagination Acts projects stands in contrast to this common reading of this text. Moreover, a reading of Pentecost where we see the gifts of difference, the blessing of many tongues also discloses how often we have chosen to seek unity through homogeneity instead of unity in the midst of such difference. Pentecost sees the people of God unified not homogenized.

And if God is present and speaking in our many languages, if God has learned the intricate syntax and particular grammar of our tongues, then our preaching, our proclamation, our prophesying should also seek to speak in many languages as well. The Spirit's speech is multiform, multilingual, multicultural.

Spirit speech today must be the same.

THEY WERE ALL TOGETHER IN ONE PLACE

The literary setting of the Pentecost scene provides important context for our reading.

The book of Acts opens with a preface that mirrors the preface of the Gospel of Luke. The narrative then takes a step back from the ending of Luke where Jesus ascends. In Acts 1, Jesus is still among the disciples after the resurrection. He is teaching and guiding still. He commissions his followers to become "witnesses" (1:8) of the gospel in geographically expanding circles from Judea all the way to the "ends of the earth," to the very edges of their cartographical imaginations. Already, difference is entering the narrative for a mission to the ends of the earth will inevitably cross cultural boundaries; the question lingering over this first chapter is what kind of mission this would be. Would it be characterized by imperial domination and homogenizing forces? Or is something beyond our imagination in view?

Jesus also makes his followers a promise. He promises that a gift is coming their way, and so they must wait in Jerusalem before taking those first steps unto the ends of the earth. As Matthew L. Skinner has pointed out, such waiting proves difficult for many of us.[3] Caught up in the Spirit's wake, we want to rush off to see where she might lead. But here Jesus asks for patience.

Jesus asks them to wait.

The gift Jesus promises arrives at Pentecost when his followers were all gathered "together in one place" (2:1b). They were all together in one place. I imagine that this is not just an indication of geography or cartography or location. The experience of the trauma of the cross, the exaltation and fear of the resurrection, and now the uncertainty of a call to the very ends of the earth means that this motley crew of disciples were together in a way deeper than location. Their hearts, we could say, are beating as one. They have met the depths of despair together. They have rejoiced in the new life of Jesus. And now they stand ready—though certainly anxious—about where the Spirit will lead them next.

We must remember too that this is the same city where Jesus was executed by the Roman Empire. This is the same city where the gospel was seen as an existential threat by the distant empire. As they huddle together, they step into the risk that they too might follow in Jesus's footsteps in a most deadly way.

They are together because they are witnesses as a community. Their very being together is a living witness of what the gospel can do. Their very unity is the gospel enfleshed. The character and tenor of that unity is about to be revealed.

AS THE SPIRIT GAVE THEM ABILITY

Suddenly, then, "tongues as of fire descend upon them" (v. 3). These tongues carry with them the power to speak in the many languages of the Jews/ Judeans gathered in Jerusalem for the festival.[4] The crowd gathered before these followers of Jesus are fellows Jews from every corner of the world. In a sense, the mandate to take the gospel to the ends of the earth is fulfilled in the opening pages of Acts for the world is already in Jerusalem. This proleptic prophetic fulfillment marks Jerusalem as the axis upon which the world turns. God's promise and call are already fulfilled the moment these followers of Jesus begin proclaiming the many languages of the world.

Here, we ought to pause to dazzle at this miracle of linguistic proliferation. Think for a moment of the difficulty of learning another language. It is not just a matter of substituting one word in a source language with another word in the target language. This is why Google Translate so often falls short of smooth translations. Language is not just about words. Language is about people and culture and place. This is why the best way to learn a language is to live somewhere the language is spoken, not just because you are forced to communicate in the language but because you are sharing the cultural air in which that language breathes and moves. Language is not just about words. Language is about food. Language is about ritual. Language is about identity.

So, we ought to be very careful about how we characterize this Pentecost moment. Notice what the Spirit has done. The Spirit has learned all our many languages. The Spirit has learned all their grammatical and syntactical oddities. The Spirit has learned every nuance of every word. The Spirit has empowered these followers of Jesus to proclaim good news in the language of our hearts. That language our mother spoke to us as babies. That language that shaped our sense of place and space and belonging. That's the language the Spirit speaks through these followers of Jesus.

Peter stands to explain to a befuddled crowd what they are seeing. Some are dazzled. Some are confused. Some simply accuse these Galileans of drunkenness at first light. But they all ask the same question, perhaps the most important question we might ask about this passage: what does this mean?

WHAT DOES THIS MEAN?

To many, Pentecost has signaled a reversal of Babel, a healing of the division Babel created, a setting right of the punishment God metes out to the arrogant builders of a tower.[5] This assumption about this text requires that we see Babel a punishment and Pentecost as its repair. This assumption also leads us to conclude that our many languages and cultures are a problem for us, an obstacle on the way to unity. Such a conclusion has misshaped our relationships to difference. I will suggest here that this is a misreading of Babel and Pentecost and our experiences of difference alike.

The story of the Tower of Babel is relatively well known among Christians. When I go to churches and ask for someone to rehearse the narrative, I hear the same basic skeleton of a story. The people of Babel decide to build a massive tower in order to make themselves like God or to challenge God's supremacy or as an outgrowth of local arrogance. God looks down upon what the residents of Babel have done and reacts harshly, destroying the tower and dispersing the people of the city. In the end, most have learned, God punishes the people of Babel by forcing them to speak different languages, thus inaugurating so many conflicts among those who speak different languages.

Turning to Genesis 11, we can see from whence this sketch of a narrative has emerged. But a closer reading of this text reveals a much more complicated narrative.[6] First, Genesis 11 is clear about the reason for the building of the city and its tower in the heavens, a reason that seems to have little to do with some plan to knock God off of God's pedestal in the clouds. Instead, Genesis observes that the people of Babel build the city, its wall, and its tower because they feared being scattered. They share the same words, and they worry that they might be spread across an unknown, unruly, dangerous world. They build a city with walls and a tower for the same reasons cities and nations do the same: the wall keeps enemies at bay, the tower provides a platform from which to see them approaching. That is, a scared group of humans do what we do when we feel most threatened. We huddle together with other people who speak like us, who look like us, who think like us.

God looks upon this city and says that nothing will now prove impossible for these people. So God confuses their languages and scatters them over the face of the earth. The question is why God does this. Our assumptions tend to point to punishment. God is afflicting the world with these many languages, but our experiences tell us that this can't be but a curse. Something else must be happening. Instead, God is still creating the world, even in ch. 11 of Genesis. The work of creation does not close with the first two chapters of Genesis. Instead, the world God wants to create is one that teems with languages and peoples and cultures. The people of Babel want to foreclose this difference not so much because they oppose God but because they fear what is in store for them in a dangerous and frightening world. God does not punish them with languages but prods them into a different kind of existence, a different kind of world, one that more closely reflects God's hopes when God commands Eve and Adam to multiply and fill the earth. God was not done creating a world of different languages, peoples, and cultures.

At least, that's how I read the text of Genesis 11. A reading that would see our multilingual world as a curse simply cannot cohere with the character of the God we have known in Scripture and in life. Moreover, I think Luke reads Genesis 11 in a similar way.

After all, Luke has Babel in view at Pentecost, but if he narrated a *reversal* of Babel, what would have happened at Pentecost? A reversal would have resulted in the followers of Jesus being able to speak *one* language, not the many languages of the Jews gathered in Jerusalem. An undoing of Babel would have resulted in the speaking of one language, perhaps the language of Babel itself or Hebrew or Aramaic or even a divinely sanctioned language perfectly capable of transmitting all the theological nuances God has always wanted us to understand. Indeed, the Spirit could have taught them a language with fine syntax, consistent grammar, elegant vocabulary. This would have certainly been a repudiation of the world Babel wrought.

Instead, the Spirit embraces the world Babel created. The Spirit learns all our languages, teaches them to the disciples and followers of Jesus and so embraces the diversity of our languages and our cultures. At Pentecost, God embraces our differences because, after all, it was God who made us this way.

Spirit speech is diverse speech. Spirit speech is multilingual speech. Spirit speech is multicultural speech. Spirit speech embraces different languages as a site of revelation and inspiration instead of a problem in need of mere translation.

God spoke our languages at Pentecost. In that way too, we see that the gospel is a profoundly embodied reality. Consider how we earlier grappled with the notion that language is not about words alone but about peoples and cultures. So, when the Spirit intercedes at Pentecost, speaking the gospel in every language gathered there, the Spirit did not just interchange words in one language for words in another language. Instead, the Spirit found words that would make sense to us. The Spirit spoke into particular cultural spaces. We don't have a single gospel at Pentecost spoken in one language but the nuances of every language in every place. At Pentecost, particularity matters to the Spirit, and particularity becomes the very site of God's revelation.

The implications of this reading of Pentecost are manifold. If God's speech is diverse speech, then spirit speech will reflect the diversity of God's people. This means that our theological conclusions are both contingent and prophetic, limited and necessary. We will have to speak boldly into our communities, knowing that we need other communities, other peoples to help us understand what we cannot understand on our own, to help us bear witness to something that the Spirit speaks into someone else's cultural space.

Spirit speech, in other words, depends on the speech of others. It leans on the conviction that others can teach us something we cannot learn or experience on our own. Spirit speech is humble in this way. Spirit speech loves our neighbors by listening to them on their own terms.

But most of all, spirit speech must be multicultural and multilingual. Spirit speech must seek voices we normally wouldn't hear, stories we wouldn't typically tell. Why? Because at Pentecost, different stories were not the problem God solved but the very means by which God made known the depth and breadth of the good news.

In the end, Pentecost inhabits, even invades, time and space. Pentecost places God's grace in our very midst, in the messiness of everyday (mis)communication. Pentecost declares our differences to be the fertile ground in which the gospel flowers. Earlier in this chapter, I pointed to the dying of languages as an example of the amplitude languages carry within their words and syntax and grammar; languages are not just collections of words but a binding agent of peoples. When the last speaker of a language dies, our grief should run deep. There is something about the extinction of a language, for in its death we don't just lose a language. We lose a whole world.

What if the kind of spirit speech Pentecost helps us imagine can revivify that which we have lost, bring back to life that which has died? What if spirit speech can bear the new life of resurrection because such speech is imbued with God's presence? And what if God is most present at that intersection of diverse languages and peoples that gathered at Pentecost? Perhaps then, at its best, spirit speech creates space again for those ways of thinking and speaking and being that were once lost but now have been found always by God and sometimes by us.

ROUNDTABLE CONVERSATION

1. Particularity Matters

Nikki: Central to your argument in this essay is the claim that particularity matters to the Spirit—not merely as a mode of translation but as "the very site of God's revelation." What would you hope that students and scholars would learn from this insight for their teaching, preaching, and community organizing?

Eric: Well, for starters, I hope that our readers will recognize the space the three of us are nurturing as a model for this kind of revelatory site. By engaging these texts and one another and by leaning into our racial, sexual, cultural, denominational, and disciplinary particularities, we are (in a sense) gathering together "in one place." As I expressed in my essay, this gathering runs deeper than geographical proximity.

A pernicious effect of the interpretations of Pentecost that I challenge is the flattening of cultural particularities in a misguided attempt at affirming community. We need to challenge the homogenization of God-talk that pervades the church and the theological academy. It is not enough for us to translate a word in one language with a word from another, or worse, to force all to speak in one language. Language is not just about words. I want students and scholars who read this essay to breathe deeply from the cultural air that continues to sustain them.

Jacob: I want to talk about the sharing of breath or Spirit at Pentecost. It seems that the sharing of air becomes a kind of foundation-without-foundation for spirit speech. On the one hand, you point to a shared trauma, a shared experience with Jesus that structures a certain sameness necessary for community. But on the other hand—and this is the place where all the magic happens—this sharing of breath is evanescent. In sharp contrast to *solid* structures (e.g., Being, language, America's imagined "greatness"), the "site" of God's revelation doesn't stick around.

We are doing this right now. We are sharing digital breath, allowing one another to speak from our unique cultural and methodological perspectives, giving space for thoughts, challenging ideas in a way that is generative, etc. I'm glad you named our gathering together "in one place" as a model for the possibility of Spirit speech. This is a potentially helpful resource for our readers.

Eric: I'm struck again by the phrase "together in one place." In our own contexts, that phrase lives in a fascinating tension. We are ever more connected one to another thanks to the devices we carry in our pockets or wear on our wrists and yet also so much more divided along political, socio-economic, racial, national lines. Yes, Spirit speech *is* carried by air/breath but such air, such breath also has a digital form for us today. The digital world allows this breath to reach innumerable people, bisecting borders and markers of difference. But it can also cleave us apart. So, again, being "together in one place" may have less to do with proximity and more to do with love. This is not to say that face-to-face encounters and relationships are unimportant but that even face-to-face moments can be suffused with hatred and division.

2. God and Monolingualism

Jacob: Eric, I love your insight that God speaks many languages, and I appreciate how you name our tendency to, in your words, "imagine a mono-lingual God who speaks the same words we do." When I read this, I can't help but think of Jacques Derrida's profound insight that his mother tongue (French) is at once his and yet not his. As a Jew from Algeria, which was under French imperial rule throughout Derrida's childhood, French was his primary language. In his book *The Monolingualism of the Other*, he helps us reflect on the ways that language imposes itself on us, structuring both the possibility of speech and the impossibility of freeing ourselves from a language's linguistic shackles.

As a native English speaker, I have inherited a way of thinking and speaking that at once allows me to speak of God *and* constrains my conceptualization of God by the limits of English itself. For instance, it is no wonder why I exhibited so much resistance to speaking of God in feminine terms (She/Her) when I first encountered this way of speaking and writing. English offers me only three ways to speak of the other: he, she, it. Surely, God is no mere object, so that left me with He or She. The absence of a divine pronoun in English did more than frustrate my conceptualization of God; it shaped my understanding of God's very identity.

Eric: This is really helpful, Jacob. It makes me ponder the limitations of doing theology when language is always already in play. Furthermore, since language is so pervasive, can you pull out one thread (say, sexism, racism, heterosexism) without destroying the tapestry, so to speak?

Nikki: We *do* know that if we pull on that thread, the whole thing comes undone. This is the reason postcoloniality has not had a deeper impact or effect on mainstream scholars' theological discourses and the realities they fashion; its critique runs too deep. It forces what I call a "resistance strategy of reading," advanced by non-mainstream scholars, which pushes against inherited texts and languages because of the way they delimit our thinking and speaking (about God).

Eric: Adding to that point, not all communities have the resources to engage a hermeneutic of suspicion. For example, some congregations that are made up of mostly white people are largely incapable of seeing the inherited effects of their language, because their experiences rarely create the kind of epistemological dissonance that draws attention to their language's dominance over their conceptualization of reality. That is why such communities should pay attention to what minoritized communities are reading in the biblical texts.

3. Naming God

Nikki: I'd like to move us to talk about the signifying capacity of theological discourse. Eric, you rightfully identify that a misshaped and misshaping theology teaches us how to be human and community participants in misshapen ways. One way that I see this manifested in contemporary God-talk is the way that theologies can tend to mask political and material realities. For instance, the way I signify "Allah" means something politically and ethnically in my specific cultural context. It troubles me that our languages mask so many of our political and ethnic commitments. "In God We Trust," for instance, presents a de-gendered, de-politicized, etc. God. Such modes of naming God erase the politics of the divine.

So, I want to ask: In what ways do we (in)appropriately become politicized on account of our monolingualism? What do we do with the "wholeness theology" embedded in the church?

Eric: These are the right questions to ask. One of the things I frequently say to my students is that they don't get the right to name another's wholeness for them. We are not the Jesus of the Gospels who can see our deepest needs and heal them. We cannot assume that our bodies are whole and those of others are in need to God's healing touch. When we do that (and we tend to do so regularly), we are not hearing other people's stories; instead, we are circumventing their lived experiences and imposing a sense of order upon them that may make sense in our eyes but may clash with what the other person needs or what God may hope for them.

Nikki: What makes wholeness intelligible? Can we only understand ourselves as whole because of our normative epistemologies (Butler)?

Jacob: It is important that we trouble the foundational myths surrounding God and difference that rest upon interpretive soils that valorize homogeneity. Hearing the two of you think together about this reminds me of one of Hélène Cixous's insights, namely, that "God" is the only proper noun that does not remain constant across languages. YHWH, Jehovah, Allah, Krishna—each of these attempts at naming God is rooted in particular languages that are only fully intelligible on the inside of those socio-symbolic structures. I wonder if the flattening of these names across cultures shares something with the violence of silence imposed by Empire. It seems that colonizing a people's language for God goes hand-in-hand with colonizing their land and the minds of their people.

4. Instincts of Empire

Nikki: That's a nice segue into something else in your essay, Eric. You write about the "instincts of empire," which aim "to mute differences for the sake of a dominant culture." Can you say more about that?

Eric: Sure. What troubles me most about the traditional readings of Pentecost—which assume that this radical intervention by the Spirit presents God as reversing or undoing God's fury against the inhabitants of Babel—is that they underwrite imperial logics. I contend that Pentecost sees the people of God unified not homogenized. We encounter Spirit speech in this pericope as multiform, multilingual, multicultural. This leads me to wonder how the Church that is inaugurated and sustained by the same Spirit could ever defend homogenized discourse.

Jacob: Now I'm saying this with my tongue firmly in my cheek, but is this not a central virtue of theological education: to enforce discursive conformity?

Eric: (laughs) Indeed. But I do not think that our seminaries, divinity schools, and schools of theology are doing this overtly. This does not mean that students, staff, and faculty of color do not experience a degree of alienation akin to that endured by colonized persons. Here is where the concept of hybridity helps my thinking and my orientation to theological education. I seek to embody a way with texts and theologies that is at once about identity and resistance.

    The Spirit embraces the world Babel created. This is the essence of my claim from the Pentecost scene. We who would speak in the tongues of the Spirit, whether from pulpit, podium, or the steps of the capital, will do so by honoring particularity as the very site of God's revelation.

Nikki: This is the point I was getting at earlier when I mentioned the limited impact of postcoloniality in theological education. Marginalized people are *already* employing a hermeneutic of suspicion. We can help them identify how they are employing that hermeneutic to bolster their communities' interests.

Jacob: There is a quote by Marx that Frantz Fanon cites at the end of his *Black Skins, White Masks.* Marx asserts that the social revolution he seeks (in his nineteenth-century sociopolitical context) cannot draw on the poetry or stories from the past. Marx eschews the nostalgia of earlier revolutions, arguing that the revolutions to come need to find their own content and modes of expression.

Nikki: I'm going to disagree with Marx on this point. I think there is something immensely powerful in the process of noticing, acknowledging, appreciating, and drawing upon strategies, narratives, and lessons practiced by our predecessors. For me, it is the poetics and creativity from my foreparents that provides strength and bolsters my own creativity. That creative work, resistance, struggle, etc. is the evidence of things unseen.

Jacob: That's great, Nikki. And your dissension names clearly what I find so instructive in Marx's statement. Those who share my demographic markers have shaped so many of the narratives and philosophies that structure our contemporary existences. I'm troubled by the "Make America Great Again" narrative, which continues to bolster white supremacy. Perhaps that's why I find so much hope and life in deconstructive approaches to texts and traditions. They allow me a way to think otherwise.

5. Contingent and Prophetic Conclusions

Jacob: Drawing this conversation to a close, I'm curious about your assertion that if God's speech is diverse speech, then Spirit speech will reflect the diversity of God's people. No problems here. But immediately thereafter you write, "This means that our theological conclusions are both contingent and prophetic, limited and necessary." I'd like to hear you flesh that out for us a bit.

Eric: What I want to emphasize here is a living tension that we will always experience in our theologizing. We can't help but to speak from a particular place. That is, we can only speak from the rich cultural soil that has shaped us. At the same time, that particular space is not *all* space, not *every* space. We always have to remember that our theologizing can be both rich and limited. Nonetheless, we are called to be prophetic: to speak in our communities and with other communities because the insights of our particular cultural spaces can be a rich resource for others and theirs is a help to us. Our Spirit speech is always *limited* in that it speaks a particular language in a particular place. Our Spirit speech is thus also *necessary* because such speech is the means by which we come to know who God is and whom God has called us to be. What if doing theology is like this? We—like the disciples huddled together in that upper room in Jerusalem—experience unity when we are able at once to look backward to the journey that has formed us and to look forward with anxious anticipation about the strange places where the Spirit will lead us and the unexpected strangers we will meet who will reshape how we think and speak about God.

NOTES

1. On hospitality and ecclesial practice, see Jessicah Krey Duckworth, *Wide Welcome: How the Unsettling Presence of Newcomers Can Save the Church* (Minneapolis: Fortress, 2013).

2. Cf. Brent A. Strawn, *The Old Testament Is Dying: A Diagnosis and Recommended Treatment* (Grand Rapids: Baker Academic, 2017).

3. Matthew L. Skinner, *Intrusive God, Disruptive Gospel: Encountering the Divine in the Book of Acts* (Grand Rapids: Brazos, 2015), 3–8.

4. The question about how to translate the Greek term *Ioudaios* is not just a lexicographical curiosity but a theologically pressing question, especially in light of the anti-Semitism—both implicit and explicit—too often present in New Testament scholarship. As Caroline Johnson Hodge, *If Sons, Then Heirs: A Study of Kinship and Ethnicity in the Letters of Paul* (Oxford: Oxford University Press, 2007), 11, has quipped, "If ever there were a can of worms in New Testament scholarship, the translation of *Ioudaios* is one." Here, I use both terms to alert the reader to these questions but will tend to opt to use the term "Jew" in the rest of the book. For a summary and persuasive approach to the translational, historical, and theological questions posed by this question, see Amy Jill Levine, *The Misunderstood Jew: The Church and the Scandal of the Jewish Jesus* (San Francisco: HarperSanFrancisco, 2006), 87–117. For additional resources, see Eric D. Barreto, *Ethnic Negotiations: The Function of Race and Ethnicity in Acts 16* (WUNT II 294; Tübingen: Mohr Siebeck, 2010), 73–80.

5. I cite just a few examples here. The study notes of the Oxford Annotated Bible suggest that the presence of the Spirit at Pentecost means that "the tower of Babel has been reversed." See Sherman E. Johnson, note on 2:4–11, in *The New Oxford Annotated Bible*, ed. Bruce M. Metzger and Roland E. Murphy (New York: Oxford University Press, 1994), 162. After noting that "Pentecost may be the most exciting and least comprehensible episode in Acts," Pervo notes that the perplexity of the crowd is "a confusion worthy of Babel" and that Pentecost is "a utopian restoration of the unity of the human race." See Richard I. Pervo, *Acts: A Commentary* (Hermeneia; Minneapolis: Fortress, 2009), 59, 61–62. Haenchen notes that Pentecost could have functioned for Luke "as the occasion when the confusion of Babel was abolished: the Spirit of Christ healing the divisions of mankind" but that Luke's theology of the Gentiles deferred this universal reconciliation until the conversion of Cornelius. See Ernst Haenchen, *The Acts of the Apostles: A Commentary* (Philadelphia: Westminster, 1971), 174. Barrett writes, "A more important OT reference is the account of Babel (Gen. 11.1–9), *the effect of which is now reversed*" (italics added). See C. K. Barrett, *Acts: A Shorter Commentary* (London: Continuum, 2002), 17. Trocmé argued that a "supernatural

Esperanto" had effectively undone the confusion Babel had once inflicted upon the world. See Etienne Trocmé, *Le 'Livre des Actes' en l'histoire* (Paris: Presses Universitaires de France, 1957), 202–6. Or as Cyril of Jerusalem argued, "The multitude of those listening was confounded; it was a second confusion, in contrast to the first evil confusion at Babylon. In that former confusion of tongues there was a division of purpose, for the intention was impious. Here there was a restoration and unity of minds, since the object of their zeal was righteousness. Through what occasioned the fall came the recovery." See Cyril of Jerusalem, Catechetical Lecture, 17.16–17, as cited in Frances Martin, ed., *Acts* (vol. 5 of *Ancient Christian Commentary on Scripture: New Testament*; ed. Thomas C. Oden; Downers Grove, IL: InterVarsity Press, 2006), 24.

6. I am particularly indebted to Theodore Hiebert, "The Tower of Babel and the Origin of the World's Cultures," *JBL* 126 (2007): 29–58, for these insights.

Chapter Two

Bold Speech: Acts 4:1–22

Jacob D. Myers

Following months of protests, President Obama invited a small group of leaders to meet with him. We remember all too well the horror of watching unarmed activists standing their ground against a militarized Ferguson, Missouri, police force following the murder of Mike Brown. One of the protestors who met with the president was Ashley Yates, cofounder of Millennial Activists United. Also invited to attend this meeting was the Reverend Al Sharpton. In the wake of that meeting, Yates tweeted:

> We sat around this table and listened to @theRevAl as he spoke of the work WE put in. He didn't know a single one of our names. He never set foot on a protest site. Never attended any actions planned by local organizers, but then he got up there and tried to praise. He walked his black ass clean out of the room without so much as an INTRODUCTION to any of us. Not a single word. We know what this movement is about: People Power. And what it's not about: Late Negroes in suits tryna cling to glory days. @theRevAl.

Sharpton responded, dismissing Yates's charge as emblematic of the petty rantings of "provocateurs."[1]

In his prescient book, *The End of White Christian America*, Robert Jones charts the rise and diminution of white Protestants' political and cultural power. Jones argues that evangelicals are struck with a kind of "homesickness for a lost parochial world," the vestiges of their former political clout. He concludes, "Their greatest temptation will be to wield what remaining political power they have as a desperate corrective for their waning cultural influence. If this happens, we may be in for another decade of closing skirmishes in the culture wars, but white evangelical Protestants will mortgage their future in a fight to resurrect the past."[2]

Throughout the 2016 presidential election, GOP leaders floundered before a kind of "legitimation crisis," to borrow Habermas's phrase. Senate majority leader Mitch McConnell and Speaker of the House Paul Ryan were particularly flummoxed by the Trump phenomenon.[3] Peering behind the rhetoric, posturing, and shenanigans, what was really at stake for the Republican Party in the 2016 presidential election was power and the preservation of what Emilie Townes labels the "fantastic hegemonic imagination."[4]

Trump's ascendancy to the highest American political office is nothing less than the manifestation of what Carol Anderson has aptly identified as "white rage." Trump is not an anomaly or an aberration. His racial vitriol merely gave voice to white fears and white fragility. Anderson writes, "The unbridled anger at Obama for having had the audacity to become president . . . cracked the fire-wall that would have kept the most suspect and unpopular incoming president in recorded history from gaining access to the nuclear codes."[5] It remains to be seen the extent to which this scorched-earth presidency will harm the lives of America's most vulnerable.

These disparate though overlapping illustrations point to a ubiquitous phenomenon across cultures and eras: *power legitimates discourse which legitimates power.* Such is structurally and necessarily tautological and solipsistic. By this I mean that power and discourse form a kind of closed loop, which reinforces each of its factors by means of the other. Those who control the metrics of knowledge and the means of communication get to decide what counts as knowledge and who is authorized to speak.[6] Discursive power structures move through history, gaining force by the interplay between power and discourse—like an electromagnet. Those in power wield the prevailing rationality and modes of discourse (which now includes Twitter, Facebook, Snapchat, etc.) to bolster their discursive regimes.

Contemporary Christ-followers face a double-bind when they seek to challenge authoritarian structures that militate against those on the margins, and particularly those on the margins of the margins. We want to speak out, but the very modes of discourse by which we would decry injustice are the same modes of discourse always already working to support those in power. As poet/essayist Audre Lorde taught us, it is an "old and primary tool of all oppressors to keep the oppressed occupied with the master's concerns" (e.g., Donald Trump's Twitter rants). In other words, as the title of Lorde's speech puts it: "The master's tools will never dismantle the master's house."[7] Regardless of our intentions, employing forms of thinking and speaking to challenge oppressive systems can end up reinforcing the very structures we would seek to supplant.

This is where Peter's discursive agency in Acts 4:1–22 becomes so instructive. Before the Sanhedrin—literally the *seat* of religious and political power (the Greek word συνέδριον means "sitting together")—Peter's speaking in verse 8 is "filled with the Holy Spirit" (πλησθεὶς Πνεύματος Ἁγίου).[8] Accordingly, Peter and John's "boldness" (παρρησία) causes the epistemological foundation of the "rulers" and "elders" to tremble (v. 13). How and to what extent such bold speech does its work will be the focus of this chapter.

We will examine this pericope in three parts: 1) Peter and John's precipitating transgression (vv. 1–4); 2) Peter's genealogical rupture of his culture's dominant epistemology (vv. 5–12); and 3) The effect and consequences of Peter's de-constructive God-talk (vv. 13–22). To support these analyses, I draw upon the work of the eminent French historian of systems of thought, Michel Foucault. Foucault's particular brand of deconstruction helps us better understand the effects of Peter's boldness and how we might exercise "bold speech" in our contemporary discursive milieus.

TRANSGRESSING SOCIOPOLITICAL STRUCTURES

Acts 4:1–22 narrates a kind of deconstruction, one that would come to rupture the fabric of the world order. Let us walk though this pericope slowly to attend to what it may teach us.

Luke begins this narrative simply enough. Peter and John are speaking (λαλούντων). We know from Acts 3 the precipitating event and matter under discussion. Peter and John have healed a paraplegic man who had been structurally excluded from the religious community. It is crucial that we tie this material act of liberation in chapter 3 to what follows in chapter 4. As James Cone teaches us, "Without concrete signs of divine presence in the lives of the poor, the gospel becomes simply an opiate; rather than liberating the powerless from humiliation and suffering, the gospel becomes a drug that helps them adjust to this world by looking for 'pie in the sky.'"[9] When challenged to make sense of this miracle, Peter proceeds to frame this act of God's concern for the marginalized within Israel's foundational narrative, their religious social imaginary, to borrow Charles Taylor's language. By the time we arrive at chapter 4, Peter and John are still speaking to the people, and their ranks have swelled to at least 5,000 people.

That Luke wishes to make a distinction between the people in general and those in power seems evident. In fact, it appears that Luke intends to bring the entire Jerusalem establishment under erasure. Here we encounter three sets of people: (1) The priests, those at the top of the religious hierarchy; (2) The captain of the temple guard, the chief enforcer of the status quo; and (3) The Sadducees, members of the political aristocracy.[10] In short, Luke has staged his narrative to challenge the very religious, legal, and political powers that had so recently colluded in Jesus' state-sanctioned murder.

Peter and John weren't just speaking with the people. One does not *speak* to 5,000 people. Luke tells us that Peter and John were teaching (διδάσκειν) and preaching (καταγγέλλειν). By these actions, they were crossing a line set by those wielding power, for—much like today—it is the ones who are in charge who adjudicate the qualifications for teaching and preaching. Peter and John were transgressing these power structures by the mere fact that they were teaching (cf. v. 13). Despite the methodological challenges of reconstructing the Sadducees' identity from later rabbinic texts, the Sadducees' commitment to maintain strict delegations of power receives much historical support.[11] But legitimizing the historical plausibility of this scene is less important for our purposes than discerning the sociopolitical significance of this act of transgression. Accordingly, Hans Conzelmann argues, "There are difficulties with this account if it is taken as a historically accurate report. Those problems disappear if we recognize it as a redactional revision of an account which can no longer be reconstructed in its original form." And, in reference to Peter and John's impropriety in teaching and preaching, "The astonishment here is not historical but literary; it provides a foil: in place of a rhetorical production appears a speech which is due to the work of the Spirit."[12] Whether this scene was historically accurate or a Lukan literary invention matters little.

The *subject matter* of their teaching bears most significantly in Luke's narration: the transgressive message that in Jesus the dead are resurrected. This is no casual aside. Later, in Acts 23:8, Luke will state explicitly that Sadducees do not believe in the resurrection.[13] Note that these leaders "were distressed" (διαπονούμενοι), both by Peter and John's transgression of socio-religious boundaries and by their talk of resurrection from the dead—so distressed, in fact, that they arrested them (vv. 2–3).[14]

Foucault helps us to get a better sense of what is taking place in the opening of this narrative. In his *Lectures on the Will to Know*, Foucault reiterates a central feature of his mode of deconstruction: the threshold. The threshold is both a site of entry and exclusion. It marks the inside from the outside, even as it creates the difference between them. This is fundamental to Foucault's project of delegitimizing the very legitimation of power, whereby the inside is created through the very act of delimiting an outside.[15] Luke stresses this distinction between those on the inside and those on the outside later in his narrative when the establishment leaders denounce Peter and John as "uneducated and ordinary men" (v. 13).

In his *Lectures*, Foucault traces the movements in the history of philosophy, wherein knowledge *(savoir)* is produced by delimiting a certain interiority that becomes inaccessible from outside the boundaries set by those who established the boundaries in the first place. The created interiority "always brings with itself a fundamental and ineradicable relation to the truth," and no discourse and no practice that is not already internal to the truth under question "can really affect it." Foucault continues, noting how knowledge/ truth is maintained through a process of *return*, whereby whatever needs to be said has always already been said. He then asks, "Where will it find what it now has to say if not in itself; if not by thinking what was still unthought in the thought already thought; if not by taking what has already been said as both the object of thought and the subject of repetition?"[16] Foucault's deconstruction crosses the (constructed) threshold, leading us to the inside. Hereby, Foucault reinscribes a return at the origin of regimes of discourse. By daring to enter into "regimes of power" at the very source of their power, he is thereby able to rupture "truth" from within.

I believe that Peter and John are performing a kind of Foucauldian deconstruction here in Luke's narrative. Through their speaking, teaching, and preaching they draw the common people (τὸν λαὸν) into Israel's socioreligious history, taking hold of the knowledge/truth that has militated against and thereby marginalized the people. This return will become even more prominent when Peter addresses the Sanhedrin in the verses that follow.

RUPTURING OPPRESSIVE EPISTEMOLOGIES

Luke takes great care to alert us to those who gather the following day in response to Peter and John's transgressive behavior: their rulers, elders, and scribes, Annas the high priest, and key members of the high-priestly family. Before this assembly Peter declares, "Let it be known to all of you, and to all the people of Israel, that in the name of Jesus of Nazareth—the one whom you crucified, the one whom God raised from the dead—this man stands before you, whole" (v. 10). There is something idiomatic about Luke's wording here (cf. Acts 1:19; 2:14; 13:38; 19:17; 28:22, 28). "Let it be known" (γνωστὸν ἔστω), Peter declares. It is at once imperative and circumlocutional. It is as if this command to know achieves its possibility beyond knowledge. It can't *be* known (γινώσκω) nor can it be an *object* of knowledge (γνῶσις). This kind of knowing without knowing is adjectival; it attaches itself to a person beyond agency, beyond culturally conditioned identities.

God's raising of Jesus from the dead is not only beyond knowledge; it ruptures the very possibility of knowledge within the reigning body's discursive frame. As Foucault teaches us, "Discursive practices are characterized by the delimitation of a field of objects, the definition of a legitimate perspective for the agent of knowledge, and the fixing of norms for the elaboration of concepts and theories. Thus, each discursive practice implies a play of prescriptions that designate its exclusions and choices."[17] God's resurrection of Jesus is beyond delimitation—particularly for the Sadducees, whose field of knowing precludes the possibility of resurrection. Furthermore, Jesus' resurrection collapses these knowers' very capacity to know. When the might and machinations of the cultural, religious, and political orders fail to reach their intended destinations—when even the biological order fails to keep dead things dead—what else might be possible? This is what Luke signals with his γνωστὸν ἔστω.

Then, in v. 11, Luke drops the bomb he's been building since the beginning of this scene (3:1): "This one is the stone, which having been utterly despised by you builders, has become the chief corner (stone)." Here Luke offers us a glimpse of what he's really up to in this pericope: rupturing the Judean epistemological order. Let me explain.

Near the end of *History of Madness*, Foucault enumerates different types of thought and language prohibited under particular discursive regimes. What we witness in Peter's speech, which so thoroughly flummoxes the epistemological gatekeepers in vv. 5–12, is one such of Foucault's types. Peter's discursive performance is the most dangerous of said types to the first-century Judean *episteme* (*viz.*, the a priori historical conditions that establish the possibility of certain kinds of thinking and speaking) because it so closely resembles it *while* transgressing it.[18] Foucault writes,

> Finally, there is a fourth form of excluded language: this consists of submitting speech that apparently conforms to the recognized code to a different code, whose key is contained within that speech itself, so that the speech is doubled inside itself; it says what it says, but it adds a mute surplus that silently states what it says and the code according to which it is said. . . . It sets itself up from the very first instant in an essential fold of speech. A fold that mines it from the inside, perhaps to infinity. What is said in such language is of little importance, as are the meanings that are delivered there. It is this obscure and central liberation of speech at the heart of itself, its uncontrollable flight to a region that is always dark, which no culture can accept immediately. Such speech is transgressive, not in its meaning, not in its verbal matter, but in its *play.*[19]

This "mute surplus," this "fold of speech" is named differently by Luke. He calls it Spirit speech (v. 8). How said speech takes shape is quite perplexing, and to get a clear sense of it we'll eventually have to pan out to look at the narrative in its entirety.

At first glance, Peter's invocation of Psalm 118:22 seems to come out of nowhere. The Sanhedrin leaders ask him, "By what power or by what name did you do this?" Luke likes to tee-up his protagonists, but here Peter swings and misses—or at least fouls it out of bounds. How does Peter get from *power* and *name* to *stones* and *builders*? How many other proof-texts could have served Luke's purpose here? Even in Psalm 118 he could have found such a text: "They surrounded me, surrounded me on every side; in the name of the Lord I cut them off" (v. 11).

What is more, Luke misquotes Psalm 118:22. We know that he knows this verse because in Luke 20:17 he provides an exact quotation of the Septuagint's rendering of the Hebrew. The most significant change that Luke makes here in chapter four by replacing the Psalmist's verb meaning "to reject" (ἀποδοκιμάζω) with the verb meaning "to utterly despise" (ἐξουθενέω).[20] Why does Luke misquote the Psalm, if not to disrupt an easy assimilation of that text into this context? Or perhaps his engagement with the Psalm challenges the very possibility of misquoting and the imagined contextual stability many mainstream biblical interpreters assume. I believe that Luke wishes to remind Peter's accusers (the chief priests and scribes, cf. Luke 23:10) of their active participation in Jesus' death, a death that has now ruptured their carefully curated sociopolitical order by God's resurrection of Jesus.

On one level, Peter is responding to a question by quoting scripture—a properly rabbinical and conventional move. On another level, out of a certain "fold of speech," we might say, Peter indicts his interrogators for Jesus' death. And that is why Peter adds in v. 12 that it is only in Jesus' name that it is possible (δεῖ) to be saved (cf. Ps 118:21, 26). Luke is subtly and carefully rupturing his accusers' epistemology—indeed, their entire power base. Ironically, this Jesus whom they cut off now makes salvation itself possible.

Emboldening Liberation

Peter speaks truth to power by subverting the a priori metrics that simultaneously sustain and delimit truth. These powerful metrics ensure that power remains with those who already have power. The powerful control the truth, and Peter and John seize power by subverting the very conditions for the possibility of truth. The power to speak the truth is internal to the speaker's discourse. If it requires commentary or any kind of extra-discursive scaffolding, it vanishes as truth. That is why the religious leaders are effectively rendered mute following Peter's Spirit speech (v. 14).

Peter and John speak with "boldness" or "self-certainty" (παρρησία), which is named as such by their accusers in v. 13. Such bold speech destabilizes dominant discursive logics by inhabiting and thereby transgressing their metrics. In other words, bold speech is perceived as such when it enters the house (bold), when it subverts the law of the house, when it brings such economics (οἶκος-νόμος) to a halt. But we are getting ahead of ourselves.

The English word *bold* enjoys a dual etymology, a kind of split personality that is displayed in Peter and John's discursive acts. On the one hand, it is adjectival, signifying boldness, confidence, and even impudence. It modifies its beholder. On the other hand, the word *bold* relates to structures (house, dwelling place, property, inheritance). Though this nominal construal is now obsolete in English, it is sustained in the verb *build*.

Bold speech builds its own house. According to its own measures and metrics. Its confidence is internal to its own manifestation. Such speech, while audible, is visible (Θεωροῦντες δὲ τὴν τοῦ Πέτρου παρρησίαν καὶ Ἰωάνου, "But seeing the boldness of Peter and John"). Bold speech transgresses the simple opposition between the aural and the visual, between sound and sight.

Once again, Foucault helps us make sense of what Luke is up to in this pericope. In 1983, Foucault delivered six lectures at the University of California at Berkeley, "Discourse and Truth: The Problematization of *Parrhesia*." In these lectures, Foucault traces the use of this word through Greco-Roman literature, noting the term's ambivalence. From the point of view of those in power, bold speech (i.e., speech that does not acquiesce to discursive regimes) presents a "crisis of truth" that is at once constitutive of and threatening to democracy.[21] When discursive acts submit to a truth that is internal to the discourse itself, it disrupts the play of power/truth that authorizes speech as such.

Following Foucault, I submit that we read v. 13 with all its semantic undecidability. Not only could we justifiably translate παρρησία as "prattling," but the word θαυμάζω could equally mean "to be amazed" or "to be perplexed" (cf. Lk 2:33; 4:22; 8:25; and 24:41). This all depends on one's discursive frame. So, whether the Sanhedrin received Peter's words as *bold* or *foolish* remains unclear in the narrative. What we do know is that the epistemological frame of the Sanhedrin could not account for the presence of this crippled man standing in their midst.

Cornell West also helps us make sense of this narrative undecidability. In his book, *Democracy Matters*, West makes great use of this word παρρησία. He links it to the democratic ideals embodied in Socrates' mode of questioning as well as the prophetic commitment to justice found in scripture. West defines παρρησία as "fearless speech," which "unsettles, unnerves, and unhouses people from their uncritical sleepwalking."[22] It exposes the specious reasoning that legitimates power structures and delimits speech. Such speech is an-archic, submitting neither to a priori metrics of knowledge nor to contemporary rule. This is what we find in Peter's Spirit speech and in Peter and John's liberating act of healing.

CONCLUSION: EMBRACING BOLDNESS

Peter's Spirit-inspired speech before the social, religious, and political powers of his day advance a mode of discourse that may inform the contemporary American context. As I write this chapter, during the week of Donald Trump's presidential victory, I am wondering about the sociopolitical ramifications of making America "great again."[23] If Trump fulfills even a fraction of the promises he made to gain the 270 electoral votes he needed, Christ-followers will require the courage to teach and preach justice. We will need boldness to challenge racist, sexist, homophobic, and xenophobic policies. The Book of Acts is a resource in this fight that we ought not dismiss.

Foucault argues that

> the essential political problem for the intellectual is not to criticize the ideo-logical contents [of a discourse] . . . but that of ascertaining the possibility of constituting a new politics of truth. The problem is not changing people's con-sciousness—or what's in their heads—but the political, economic, institutional regime of the production of truth.
>
> It's not a matter of emancipating truth from every system of power (which would be a chimera, for truth is already power), but of detaching the power of truth from the forms of hegemony, social, economic, and cultural, within which it operates at the present time.[24]

Such work is not easy. What we find in Acts 4:1–22 offers a way of "detach-ing" the power of truth from is discursive manifestations. Peter's discursive acts work to transgress, rupture, and liberate truth from power. Foucault will label this kind of work genealogical.

Genealogy in Foucauldian parlance is "a form of history which can ac-count for the constitution of knowledges, discourses, domains of objects, etc., without having to refer to a subject which is either transcendental in relation to the field of events or runs in its empty sameness throughout the course of history."[25] Thus it is not so much about content as it is about questioning the governing assumptions that underwrite such content. Accordingly, genealogi-cal deconstruction does not merely refute old errors or recover of old truths. It does not aim to renew old paradigms or modify outmoded systems. Rather, such "is a question of what *governs* statements, and the way in which they *govern* each other so as to constitute a set of propositions which are scien-tifically [or theologically] acceptable."[26] Such deconstruction is far-sighted, looking past contemporary discursive acts to interrogate their very possibil-ity. Those with eyes to see, let them look.

ROUNDTABLE CONVERSATION

1. Context Matters

Eric: Two broad but related thoughts came to me as I read this chapter. First, how do we keep the book relevant to this moment but not read like a time capsule?

The thinking that we are doing here is rooted in the current political and cultural situation. How might someone read and understand this book differently in a few years when things have shifted? So, what does it mean for us to draw on the words of thinkers who have preceded us? How is it possible for us to distinguish between hearing our own thoughts from our respective contexts and experiences and quoting folks—like Foucault—who are speaking to their own contexts? Is it more important to prioritize our voices (meaning you, Nikki, and me) or the voices of other interlocutors?

Nikki: Context *is* important. It is vital to name where we are now and why this matters. Setting the stage is key, as we mentioned in the introduction. Remember, our hope was to prioritize, or at least frame, our own voices within the text. We learn about our disparate theological perspectives through descriptions of our positions and contexts as well as the responses to those descriptions that emerge in our writing.

Jacob: I try to enter into the text obliquely, that is, in a way that it opens up conversations that are emerging in my mind. I know that this chapter on bold speech is theory-heavy, and I could diminish that stuff, but I wonder if it would still teach the kind of thinking that I do. Thinking *with* people is important. But I don't just read with *anybody*. As a mostly straight, currently able-bodied, cisgender, white man, readings from folks like me have tended to assert themselves over those of other reading communities. Reading scripture alongside a thinker like Foucault displaces my dominance over texts and interpretations. My hope is that such displacement can teach and model a mode of engagement that may inform sermon development as well as more scholarly engagements with the biblical text.

Eric: That's so helpful. The second thought I had was about whether or not we should talk about different ways to do exegesis and how we read with other people. How do we use other tools like pop culture, for example?

Jacob: Both reading alongside others and engaging our contemporary cultural realities are central to my vocation. I find pop culture to be an invaluable tool for helping folks understand the hermeneutical strategies I find life-giving. My book on biblical interpretation and my book on homiletical theology, for instance, both draw upon numerous pop culture sources. From Jay-Z to J. K. Rowling, from *Game of Thrones* to *Moana*, and from *Talladega Nights* to *Gangnam Style*, I engage a range of cultural sources to illustrate my (*eh-hem*) somewhat abstruse philosophical musings.

Nikki: I like that. And, as an ethicist, I'm always trying to "ruin" the text! That is, I am interested in illustrating how the text's complexity makes room for possibilities—of thoughts, emotions, behaviors—rather than advocating stability. Such a process allows for a reflection on our own investments, motivations, fears, hopes, values, etc. That's what drives my exegetical framing, which is why I think it's so important for us to constantly notice and acknowledge our different disciplinary and theological postures towards exegesis.

Jacob: Well, it is clear from our conversations thus far that we (you, Eric, and I) agree on the epistemology-as-construction idea, which is why Lorde is so important. Part of this work, even as we chart new territory, is to recognize the tenuousness of our ways of knowing and how these ways of knowing are culturally situated. The notion of a "hermeneutical circle" affirmed by a number of liberation theologians and ethicists is helpful here because it is a very Anglo-masculine idea that we are building something—in our reading, interpreting, and writing—that lasts for millennia. We can't believe in that anymore.

Eric: We are not doing a theory of everything because that's an impossible task. Plus, it's arrogant and unhelpful! What if focusing on the here and now is the truest way of doing theology?

Jacob: I agree. Part of what we must do is make it clear that we expect that someone will come along later and notice the structural spots that we miss in the now. Trusting that this will happen allows us to recognize different ways the Spirit is embedded and invested in our encounters and engagements with the text. And in the process, we'll remember that all of this, too, is a construct. So then, my bold speech (today) can be new, but this newness will also harden to become a foundation upon which another person will need to do the necessary work of deconstruction.

2. Spirit and (or in) Action

Eric: I think this chapter helps us to think about the character of our own bold-ness in speaking about God and the assurance that the Spirit is a critical source of such boldness.

Jacob: It's easy to think ourselves bold; however, from another's point of view we may seem utterly banal. That's why reading in community is so important for me. We can see things that others can't see in their own stuff and vice versa. We can be bold to say that this structure does not participate in the life-giving work of the Spirit. That's what Peter is doing in this pericope, I think. In this way, bold speech is sort of future-oriented, yet it must remain alert to the dis-tinction between "the Saying" and "the said" (Levinas). Bold speech has a short shelf life . . . it doesn't keep.

Nikki: I'll co-sign that and add this: The speech is not just audible and visible but active! There is something about agency that we ought to lift-up here. I think it is supremely important to be able to perceive in the space between the here-and-now and the not yet. The confidence that it takes to be situated where you are, recognizing and being fine with the shifting that might occur later, is a virtue to be cultivated. Such situatedness that bears the simultaneity of stability and possibility, history and perpetuity, sacred memories and prophecies. That kind of work is spiritually and psychologically important and points to the tem-porary nature of the context that generates theological discourse.

Jacob: Right. Everything we are talking about is kinetic, not static.

Eric: Agency is an important notion. What is the nature of this agency? It's not just the boldness of the singular prophet who speaks loudly and assertively. Instead, it's an agency that is funded by other people calling you to prophetic acts. That is, it's not just speaking *for* or *to* the community but *in* and *with* people. This kind of agency is therefore not static or absolute. There's a give and take within that kind of agency. That kind of agency is relational.

Jacob: Exactly! I can't just write about ways of preaching if I can't do them myself. My style of preaching aims to perform my own deconstruction, not in self-abnegation but a stripping bare of myself before the text. Or, think about Paul Ricoeur's use of *dépouillement*—and the notion of self-emptying that makes room for something/someone to be present/known.

Nikki: Indeed. This is quite similar to Simone Weil's discussion of attention.

3. Agency, Identity, and . . . Power!

Nikki: I want to push on something. The fact that you, Jacob, are able to do that [self-emptying process] specifically has to do with your experience of power (the combination of maleness, whiteness, etc. that theologically tells you that you are okay). Making room for the spirit is itself made possible because you are already given moral agency. Better yet, our culture and this religion attributes moral agency *to you.* Your bold speech is funded by the fact that someone always already recognizes your subjectivity. Your agency is and has been confirmed. And, more than that, it has been sanctioned over and over in multiple contexts.

Eric: That's a great point. So how do we imagine boldness for people whose personhood is not recognized or seen?

Jacob: There is a prominent strand in theology and ethics (à la Niebuhr) to view humanity's greatest flaw as pride/hubris. By this reasoning, a way to lean into God/Jesus is to divest ourselves of such power. This, of course, presupposes that one *has* power. Yes, Jesus was humble; but what I also see Jesus doing in his walk to the cross is *bold* because in certain respects he doesn't have power. It is indeed a decision that I make to read texts in a non-dominant/dominating mode. But this is like the horizon for me: even as I move toward it, I never arrive *at it.* One can never be humble enough.

Nikki: I'm with you on that last bit, but what androcentric hubris to state humanity's greatest flaw! Feminist and Womanist theologians and ethicists have challenged this notion with vigor. Consider early voices that emerged—Valerie Saiving and Barbara Hilkert Andolsen, who talked about the androcentricity that bolsters a perspective that pride is all of humanity's issue. The need for boldness—a sense of self that builds on a foundation of pride, self-love, self-value and worth—is a need that we cannot separate from gender constructs, they argued. This is also true for race, sexuality, and other social identity categories. For some of us the work begins with *establishing our humanity*. Skipping this step and thinking about one's human relation with the divine is quite a privilege and not one that we (co-authors of this book) should ignore.

Eric: Can you have the latter without the former? Can you be bold without having first established your humanity? What if bold speech is made possible only if we grant ourselves a divine sense of (divine) power? Are we running away from saying that the only thing that makes such speech possible is power?

Jacob: This gets me excited: the impossible. Homiletics exists to show people how to do an impossible thing! I want to take away all the conditions of possibility. If I can do it all by myself, why do I need God? Why do white affluent churches need God at all? This is the problem with these texts: when we read a story, we tend to identify with the protagonist. When we read this text, it's easy for me to say that I'm just like Peter. I'm going to claim this bold speech for myself and my community. But this is a false parallel, because if I were honest about the power I wield by virtue of my race, gender identity, sexual orientation, class, etc., I should be aligning myself with the Sanhedrin. Acts 4 can empower/liberate all to embrace Peter's Spirit-fueled boldness, but it's important to name that we don't occupy a neutral plane of cultural existence.

Nikki: Then it's okay for us to say that we don't all need the same thing. Sin isn't the same for everyone nor is redemption. What we are calling "bold" can be different for different people?

Eric: And people don't know that because we tend to read the Bible with people who look and think like us! Western epistemologies have misshaped us.

Nikki: Well, that and the reality of colonialism. What if the boldness is not the deconstructive work but our insistence of our own humanity as the only means by which we can read the text? We refuse to ignore or erase our humanity.

NOTES

1. Cited in Eddie S. Glaude, Jr., *Democracy in Black: How Race Still Enslaves the American Soul* (New York: Crown Publishers, 2016), 181.

2. Robert P. Jones, *The End of White Christian America* (New York: Simon & Schuster, 2016), 221.

3. As of the time of this writing, the divisiveness between Ryan and McConnell arises out of two very different tactics for restoring GOP cultural and political unity. McConnell wants to retain a GOP majority in the Senate, largely in order to further his SCOTUS obstructionism in the wake of Antonin Scalia's death in January, 2016. Ryan, on the other hand, seems to be harnessing his political capital to position himself as a party unifier and 2020 Republican presidential nominee. See Rachael Bade

and Burgess Everett, "Why Ryan and McConnell Split over Trump," *Politico*, last modified October 12, 2016, http://www.politico.com/story/2016/10/paul-ryan-mitch -mcconnell-donald-trump-229629.

4. See Emilie M. Townes, *Womanist Ethics and the Cultural Production of Evil* (New York: Palgrave Macmillan, 2006). She explains, "The fantastic hegemonic imagination traffics in people's lives that are caricatured or pillaged so that the imagination that creates the fantastic can control the world in its own image" (21).

5. Carol Anderson, *White Rage: The Unspoken Truth of Our Racial Divide* (London and New York: Bloomsbury, 2016), 170.

6. Michel Foucault, *"Society Must Be Defended": Lectures at the Collége de France, 1975–1976*, ed. Arnold I. Davidson, trans. David Macey (New York: Picador, 2003), 24. "My problem is roughly this: What are the rules of right that power implements to produce discourses on truth? Or: What type of power is it that is capable of producing discourses of truth that have, in a society like ours, such powerful effects?"

7. Audre Lorde, "The Master's Tools Will Never Dismantle the Master's House," in *Sister Outsider: Speeches and Essays*, rev. ed. (New York: Crown Publishing, 2007), 110–13. The citation is from page 113.

8. The word πλησθείς is a passive aorist participle, lit. "having been filled." In other words, said filling *has been done* to Peter: a prior work, without definite duration, at work in the present. This will become crucial as my argument progresses.

9. James H. Cone, *The Cross and the Lynching Tree* (Maryknoll, NY: Orbis Books, 2011), 155.

10. As E. P. Sanders puts it, "I do not assume that all aristocrats were Sadducees, but I do assume that all or almost all Sadducees were aristocrats." *Judaism: Practice & Belief 63 BCE–66 CE* (London: SCM Press, 1992), 332. Recent scholarship has problematized historical and sociopolitical reconstructions of first-century Jewish leaders mentioned in Acts. For one, most of what we know about groups like the Pharisees and Sadducees comes from their opponents (e.g., the Gospel writers, Josephus) or later Rabbinic writers who are hundreds of years removed from this world. Second, archeological discoveries have placed earlier conclusions into question, leading to "a profound historical agnosticism." Steve Mason, "Chief Priests, Sadducees, Pharisees and Sanhedrin in Acts," in *The Book of Acts in Its Palestinian Setting*, ed. Richard Bauckham (Grand Rapids: Eerdmans, 1995), 116. See also Anthony J. J. Saldarini, *Pharisees, Scribes and Sadducees in Palestinian Society* (Grand Rapids: Eerdmans, 2001), 298, and Wayne O. McCready, "Sadducees and Ancient Sectarianism," *Religious Studies and Theology* (May 1992): 80. Even Sanders, who is opposed by many later interpreters, writes, "An actual history cannot be written, and especially not for the Sadducees" (317). Jacob Neusner, *The Rabbinic Traditions about the Pharisees before 70*, vol. 3 (Leiden: E.J. Brill, 1971), 239–40, argues that the rabbinic House-tradition, "while thematically apt to be authentic, is very likely in the first instance the creation of early Yavneh."

11. The rabbis were "extremely consistent in portraying the Sadducees as holding stricter views than the rabbis," and that this extended to the division between themselves and the laity. Eyal Regev, "The Sadducees, the Pharisees, and the Sacred:

Meaning and Ideology in the Halakhic Controversies between the Sadducees and Pharisees," *The Review of Rabbinic Judaism* 9 (2006): 127–28. Regev continues, "The strictness of the Sadducees appears time and time again throughout the Rabbinic corpus. The rabbis could scarcely invent it or increase it. They would have gained nothing from such a fabrication; indeed, it would have suggested that, in their leniency, the rabbis war less devoted to the Torah than the Sadducees." Toward the end of this essay, he writes, "Thus, the Pharisaic-Rabbinic social system is individualistic in comparison to the hierarchic one of the Sadducees" (140).

12. Hans Conzelmann, *A Commentary on the Acts of the Apostles*, Hermeneia, ed. Eldo Jay Epp with Chistopher R. Matthews, trans. James Limburg, A. Thomas Kraabel, and Donald H. Juel (Minneapolis: Fortress Press, 1987), 32, 33.

13. I find the argument of Viviano and Taylor compelling, namely, that Acts 23:8 should be read appositively, that is, "the Sadducees say that there is no resurrection, either as an angel or as a spirit; but the Pharisees acknowledge both." See Benedict T. Viviano, OP, and Justin Taylor, SM, "Sadducees, Angels, and Resurrection (Acts 23:8–9)," *Journal of Biblical Literature* 11, no. 3 (Fall 1992): 496–98. Josephus supports this assertion. In *The Wars of the Jews*, 2.165, and *The Antiquities of the Jews*, 18.16, in *Josephus: The Complete Works*, trans. William Whiston (Nashville: Thomas Nelson, 1998), 729 and 572.

14. Foucault argues that transgression is not a denial of the dominant discourse and its concomitant values, nor is it an affirmation of something new. Rather, transgression in a Foucauldian frame moves dominant discourse to its limits. He writes, "Transgression carries the limit right to the limit of its being; transgression forces the limit to face the fact of its imminent disappearance, to find itself in what it excludes." Michel Foucault, "A Preface to Transgression," in *Language, Counter-Memory, Practice: Selected Essays and Interviews*, ed. Donald F. Bouchard, trans. Donald F. Bouchard and Sherry Simon (Ithaca, NY: Cornell University Press, 1977), 34.

15. Gilles Deleuze hits the mark when he writes that "in all of his work Foucault seems haunted by this theme of an inside which is merely the fold of the outside, as if the ship were a folding of the sea." Gilles Deleuze, *Foucault*, ed. and trans. Seán Hand (London and New York: Continuum, 2006), 80.

16. Michel Foucault, *Lectures on the Will to Know: Lectures at the Collège de France, 1970–1971*, ed. Daniel Defert, trans. Graham Burchell (New York: Palgrave Macmillan, 2013), 38.

17. Foucault, "History of Systems of Thought," in *Language, Counter-Memory, Practice,* 199.

18. In *The Order of Things: An Archeology of the Human Sciences* (New York: Vintage Books, 1994), xx–xxii, Foucault characterizes *episteme* thusly:

> The fundamental codes of a culture—those governing its language, its schemas of perception, its exchanges, its techniques, its values, the hierarchy of its practices—establish for every man [*sic*], from the first, the empirical orders with which he will be dealing and within which he will be at home. . . . I am not concerned, therefore, to describe the progress of knowledge towards an objectivity in which today's science can finally be recognized; what I am attempting to bring to light is the epistemological field, the *episteme* in which knowledge, envisaged apart from all criteria having reference to its rational value

or to its objective forms, ground its positivity and thereby manifests a history which is not that of its growing perfection, but rather of its conditions of possibility.

19. Foucault, *History of Madness*, 545.

20. NB. Luke employs this latter word to describe Jesus' mistreatment by Herod's soldiers in Luke 23:11.

21. Addressing the term's historical ambivalence, Foucault writes, "Democracy by itself is not able to determine who has the specific qualities which enable him or her to speak the truth (and thus should possess the right to tell the truth). And *parrhesia*, as a verbal activity, as pure frankness in speaking, is also not sufficient to disclose truth since negative *parrhesia*, ignorant outspokenness, can also result." "Discourse and Truth: The Problematization of *Parrhesia*," lecture 6, accessed November 13, 2016, http://foucault.info/documents/parrhesia/.

22. Cornell West, *Democracy Matters: Winning the Fight against Imperialism* (New York: Penguin Group, 2004), 16–17.

23. NB: "One should totally and absolutely suspect anything that claims to be a return. . . . History preserves us from the sort of ideology of the return." Foucault, "Space, Knowledge, and Power," in *A Foucault Reader*, 250.

24. "Truth and Power," in *A Foucault Reader* 74–75.

25. Ibid., 59.

26. Ibid., 54. Said differently, "If intellectuals in general are to have a function, if critical thought itself has a function, and, even more specifically, if philosophy has a function within critical thought, it is precisely to accept this sort of spiral, this sort of revolving door of rationality that refers us to its necessity, to its indispensability, and at the same time, to its intrinsic dangers." Foucault, "Space, Knowledge, and Power," 249.

Chapter Three

Prophetic Speech: Acts 10:34–48

Thelathia "Nikki" Young

One of the most powerful things about God-talk in the New Testament is that it illustrates the divine capacity to deconstruct the socio-political systems that underwrite oppression. Peter's speech in Acts 10:34–48 confronts and resists such a system within the early church by prescribing a new vision for human relations. While readers may understand Luke's work in these verses as a delineation of what the church should look like and how people within the church must see themselves and one another, we may also recognize Luke's effort to trouble and transform the main characters' subjectivity.

This chapter focuses on the process and product of divine imagination, social construction, and world-making. Using Peter's speech, I think about how the Holy Spirit's presence results in new ways of perceiving and speaking about the world, and I consider what kind of world the speech creates. In such a world, new subjects and subject relations exist. I also explore the simultaneity of particularity and nonpartiality, showing that Peter's speech calls for an eradication of inequality but *not* the dismissal of difference. The chapter also includes an interrogation of the power and politics of moral subjectivity and agency, both within the context of Peter's speech and in the current social and political climate of the United States.

Peter's speech contributes to the construction of a new world—a world that Jesus projected—in which God's acceptance is universal and unrelated to identity. The utterance is about divine social construction and the cultivation of a new social context. Such a construction shifts subject relations, and in so doing alters moral subjectivity while also calling for Holy Spirit–driven moral agency. The Holy Spirit, which "fell upon all who heard," requires them to speak differently about the world (Acts 10:44). It makes them imagine a future that disrupts hierarchies based on an assumption of divine partiality; the Holy Spirit makes them equals. So, through Peter, Luke has as much to say about the *persons* who constitute the church as it does about the value of equality *within* the church that underwrites human relations. But what the text does NOT do is erase particularity in the service of supporting this notion of nonpartiality. Instead, it shows how universalism, the cultivation of a collective, is still possible with the presence of difference. What is required in the new world—the imagined future—is that people recognize and understand their subjectivity and subject relations through the context of divine declaration.

DIVINE SOCIAL CONSTRUCTION
AND IMAGINATIVE WORLD-MAKING

The work of imagination entails conceiving new worlds and creatively generating the matter of such a place. The production of different kinds of life forms constitutes social construction through the work of divine speech. For example, a world that was once formless and empty became filled with lightness and darkness, heavens, water, creatures, vegetation, and more (Gen. 1:1–27; Gen. 2:4–24). By constructing new matter, the creative gods imagined new contexts and new social possibilities. In creating subjects, actions, and expectations, God-talk shaped relations of capacity, access, and power.

In this way, then, imagining and constructing new worlds is queer work. Its queerness resides in the absurd (non-rational) simultaneity of what *is* and what *can be*. The perceptive and experiential capacity to exist in the *now* and the *not yet* shatters the binary of time, disrupts the division between reality and possibility, and emancipates the future from the limits of the present. The gods of the creation stories existed in one reality while imagining and naming new ones. It was divine queer social constructions that formulated longstanding notions of intelligence, relations, labor, and power; it was a moral invention.

Queer constructions of social contexts and possibilities are moral endeavors that simultaneously evoke, invoke, and provoke realities. Not only does queer work confront, disrupt, and subvert normativity, but it also *drives* imagination. By occupying the nebulous space between what is known and what is make-believe, queer creative action forces us to recognize that the realities and contexts that we construct reflect our fantastical motivations. That is, our inventions reflect our investments. Queerness pulls back the veil on unspoken and hegemonic values that underwrite systems of morality; it removes any attempt to deny that imaginative work is moral work.

In *Black Queer Ethics, Family, and Philosophical Imagination*, I describe moral imagination as "a process of emotional, rational and active conscientizing."[1] I suggest that this frame of imagination moves beyond illusory visioning toward creative transformation. It ushers us toward futures dripping with new, liberated social possibility because it substantiates our efforts to respond rationally, emotionally, and actively to possibilities that inhibit our capacity to flourish. This double focus on reality and possibility is central to our capacity to both transform what *is* and form what is *not yet*.

Luke is doing something similar in Peter's speech. As Jews and Gentiles made meaning over time about the differentiation in power and access to divine resources, they were co-creating and living into a world built on subjective difference and social hierarchy. Peter's speech heralds a new use of moral imagination. He *de*constructs and dismantles the social relations that shape the context in which the new faith community resides, thereby subverting relational norms.

It is important to note the context of this speech. In the beginning of the chapter, Luke introduces the idea of a new world and new relations in his description of Peter's vision. In the space of the vision, Peter faces a decision about following the laws that establish righteous action in relation to cleanliness or to listening to what God commands. The latter is connected to the transformation of fowl: what God has called clean is, in fact, no longer profane (Acts 10:15). The construction of the fowl's cleanliness marks a necessarily new relation, a new subject position for Peter. The transformation that we witness, then, has to do with Peter's capacity to properly identify (and act in relation to) beings set before him. Moreover, the vision functions as an indication that divine speech is more important (and authoritative) than previously established social proscriptions. Listening to God, Luke illustrates, may entail violating relational boundaries.

Luke troubles the meaning of subject relations by describing the meeting between Peter and a Gentile centurion named Cornelius. A new convert within the community, Cornelius epitomizes the complexity of social identity that shapes human relations during this period. In connecting their meeting with Peter's visions of newly clean fowl, Luke invites readers to consider the importance of Cornelius' conversion on one hand, and *Peter's* conversion on the other. As Cornelius is "made clean," the boundary between him and Peter dissipates. In this way, Peter's meeting with Cornelius is a site and moment that illustrates a shift in social relations through the transformation of both persons' subjectivity.

So, at the start of Peter's speech, readers are already embedded within a narrative that illustrates a transformative encounter. Luke's description of a changed fowl and converted soldier, concurrent with a change in Peter's relation to both, depicts an important shift in perspective that is based on God's command. The body of the speech contains Peter's short version of the gospel, which also alludes to significant changes. Paralleling his earlier work, Luke establishes what was familiar to those who were gathered by having Peter call on listeners to remember the "message [God] sent to the people of Israel" (Acts 10:36). Just like Peter knew the fowl and how to relate to it (and Gentiles and how to relate to them), the people knew the story of the gospel and what it meant for their lives. And, in keeping with the command about the fowl's cleanliness and an obligatory visit to Cornelius, God-talk interjects into what is known, as Peter announces, "He commanded us to preach to the people and to testify that . . . everyone who believes in him receives forgiveness of sins through his name" (Acts 10:42–43).

Just after Peter draws on current perceptible realities and shared understandings of personhood and social relations, he mentions baptism. Baptism precedes the message that "spread throughout Judea" (Acts 10:37), changing the world in which they lived. Therefore, its inclusion in this part of the speech marks a coming shift in spatial, temporal, and relational reality. Such a shift is a perceptual one, as Peter wants listeners to recall realities before and after Jesus' baptism. Before, many people were oppressed by the devil (Acts 10:38); after, all who believed would be released from the oppression of sin *and* gain access to God's acceptance (Acts 10:35, 43). In other words, the release from oppression changes relationships with God and others. Thus, Peter's speech is a kind of kaleidoscope, transforming shared perceptions about the social context and altering social relations and power dynamics. This alteration of social relations and power dynamics *is* the creation/construction of a new world.

THE HOLY SPIRIT, NEW SPEECH, AND NEW WORLDS

Luke couples Peter's imaginative speech with the presence of the Holy Spirit, whose agency is made evident by the speaking of tongues. In these verses, new speech meets new speech. When Peter takes listeners through their faith history, he drops them off in a place that is wholly unknown. Though "they put him to death on a tree" (Acts 10:39), God freed Jesus from the oppression of death (v. 40). In the simple retelling of their shared narrative, Peter shows them that the world about which he is speaking is so new, so unimagined, that it even dismantles the line between life and death. Such shattering, he reminds them, is the power of perceiving and speaking differently about the world.

Black queer realities are also products of imagination and new speech. One of the first scholars I turn to when exploring the relationship between imagination, new worlds, and black queer livability is José Muñoz. His notion of a queer utopia draws on a paradigm of survival familiar in queer-of-color conceptualizations, as his work points towards hope and possibility that subverts the normativizing and hostile context of the United States. In *Cruising Utopia*, Muñoz illustrates the parallel between queer of color realities as new possibilities and imagined futures and identities as malleable. Discussing disidentificatory performance and its world-making power, Muñoz suggests that imagining new subjectivities, social relations, and political contexts is more than the offering of queer critique of present realities.[2] Instead, it is the process of imagining (and then performing) disruptive behaviors that generate counter-hegemonic discourse and action. This countering is transformative in that it draws on the dismantled (and disheveled) pieces of normative contexts and reconstitutes them through the agential process of creative, liberated social construction.

The example of black queer survival in the normativizing and hostile context of the United States, which I highlight in my book, shows how people inhabit spaces of social and subjective reality that are being both altered and created. By loving themselves and one another, by creating and shaping families with their own value systems, by refusing to be ameliorated by the death-dealing power of capitalist-driven assimilation and self-denial, black queers are transforming realities and constructing worlds before our eyes. Even more, in the current context of violent policing and the ongoing systemic destruction of black livability, the suggestion that black lives matter is a crucial work of our collective imagination; it is literally an engagement with science fiction—the *actual* creation of a make-believe future.

Here again, imaginative work uses the simultaneity embedded in queerness to doubly focus on fostering alterity to what is tangible and present and generating newness based on possibilities. When imagination manifests in worldmaking, it "engenders worlds of ideological potentiality that alter the present and map out the future."[3] In the same way, *moral* imagination does not leave our realities, experiences, and motivations in some forgotten past; instead, it honestly and intentionally recognizes how those elements (can) contribute to the new worlds. Additionally, it sets a game plan for challenging some aspects of our world that we may want to alter. Alterity, then, becomes both a component of the transformed future and a lens for perceiving the present.

When the Holy Spirit falls "upon all" *as* Peter is speaking (Acts 10:44), it is the *present* that changes. In the moment, there is a shift in agency, in the capacity to speak. The circumcised believers watch a sacred transformation— the Gentiles receiving and acting upon the Spirit's gift (Acts 10:45)—happen in real time. "Speaking in tongues" (Acts 10:46), the Gentiles are likewise experiencing and co-creating a new world in the moment. In this new world, all are welcome participants of divine gifts; all are able to perceive and speak about the world anew. The world that Peter's speech imagines, along with the perceptual shifts required to exist in such a place, manifest before all who are gathered. They realize that the result of the Holy Spirit's work is equal access to the sacred ritual of creating community.

With the elimination of partiality between the circumcised and the uncircumcised, the Holy Spirit's arrival troubles the stability of identity, giving way to new subjectivity and a new sense of agency. Let's be clear: this new speech is not random; it exists in a way that privileges community and connection. The Gentiles are not speaking an unknown language or simply making noise. They are, instead, speaking in ways that are newly intelligible, despite apparent boundaries of social difference. In this way, the Holy Spirit's gift of "tongues" allows new subjects to speak *to* and be in communion *with* one another.

PARTICULAR SUBJECTS IN A NON-PARTIAL WORLD

Luke's emphasis on inclusiveness and shaping a cohesive community does not begin with but *continues* in Peter's speech, since the Holy Spirit has already been at work. For example, Luke describes Phillip's meeting and baptism with the Ethiopian Eunuch (read: black queer) on the road to Gaza, which constituted the first Gentile conversion (Acts 8:26–40). Literally hailing from "the end of the earth" (Acts 1:8), the Ethiopian Eunuch represents both the extremity of Gentile otherness and shifting possibilities of identity. Immediately following this story, Luke narrates Saul's encounter with Jesus on the road to Damascus as well as his subsequent Spirit-filled baptism (Acts 9:1–18). Once Saul recovered from having lost his sight (Acts 9:18–19), he began to speak differently. When Saul spoke in the synagogue, people were amazed (ἐξίσταντο) (Acts 9:21).

We see ἐξίσταντο appear in Acts 10:45, when the circumcised people see the Gentiles speaking in tongues. Here, we see ἐξίσταντο translated as "astounded." In both instances, the translation signals to the readers that people who heard new speech were, in some significant way, surprised. Yet, I find that the term's first definition is equally as useful and possibly more appropriate, as it indicates a shifting of the subject. The people hearing and witnessing new speech are "thrown out of position," not just in their perspective, but also in their subjectivity. They can no longer relate to one another in the same ways because the boundaries between them have fallen away.

Thus, what we are witnessing through Luke's stories in Acts are continual shifts in subject position, brought on by significant encounters and sealed with the Holy Spirit's presence during baptism. These shifts in subject position are markers of the new world and the new community that Peter describes. The community of faith requires movement and transformation, and it is predicated upon new and particular subjects.

Once Peter understands the transformation in relational boundaries (which occurred when the Holy Spirit fell upon all as he was still speaking (Acts 10:44), he returns to his thesis. He does not suggest that those who receive the Holy Spirit are now the same as one another in terms of identity. Instead, Peter notes that the Holy Spirit's presence removes any reason to withhold baptism. Here lies a significant difference. The Greek is nicely ambiguous in its use of the phrase ὡς καὶ ἡμεῖς. The translation "just as we have," leaves us to wonder if Peter is saying one of two equally important things. On one hand, he may simply be suggesting that the Gentiles received the Holy Spirit just like the circumcised folks did. This understanding suggests a breaking of boundaries in terms of access to God's gifts and falls in line with Luke's descriptions of baptisms and conversions. On the other hand, Peter may use "just as we have" to mean "as we have done in the past." Such an interpretation illustrates a shift in behavior on the part of circumcised believers. In either case, God is not partial. God places no value on their subjective difference and "shows no partiality" by accepting all who believe (Acts 10:34). The reality of God's impartiality reframes human relations and solidifies the foundation of the new community of believers.

THE POWER AND POLITICS OF MORAL AGENCY

This point is not lost on Luke. World-creation can be potentially as individually destructive as it is collectively productive. That is, once Jesus' world-creation efforts—a political endeavor from the start—really took off, *he* became the target of political suppression (cf. Luke 11:37–54; Luke 16:14–17). During Peter's recounting of the gospel, Luke reminds readers that a possible result of being a moral agent who challenges and dismantles the system is "hanging . . . on a tree" (Acts 10:39). Establishing new social relations, political and economic systems, and communities, Luke suggests, is costly; it requires investments . . . and sacrifices. In addition to his great work of "healing all who were oppressed" (Acts 10:38), Jesus' very own life was a part of the material investment in the divinely imagined future.

We can see this truth mirrored in an American context today in the way blackness is a necessary sacrifice for unjust American social, political, and economic set of relations. Blackness—and by extension, black people—are not (nor have we ever been) a part of the American future. Blackness and black people have only existed as part of the American moral trajectory as objects in service of the production of a future. The moral framework that drives American liberal democratic hopes is based on a white moral imaginary that never included black people as moral subjects. This framework relegates to the margins cis-women, queer and transfolks, disabled folks, poor folks, and folks who sit at the intersections of multiple of these and other identity vectors to an adjectival and unnecessary existence. This kind of ethical framework is why many white liberals find it easy to look past the socially and politically sanctioned use of black bodies as sacrificial material for the collective good.

For Luke, the collective good of the new community would not require the continued practice of sacrificing (or ignoring, marginalizing, erasing, dehumanizing) some for the sake of the other. By doing away with previous limitations, it would be a new, revolutionary counter-public that defies the logic of subjective hierarchical categorization. Peter reminds all who were gathered that Jesus' story did not end with his sacrifice through public lynching. "God raised [Jesus] on the third day," *after* he had been put to "death" (Acts 10:40). Previously imagined and predicted, Jesus' resurrection—his resistance to the rules and constraints of death—was a part of the community's new reality. So earthshaking was the power of world-making that it could shatter even such "permanent" and polarized contexts/realities as life and death. Moreover, this new world and community demanded the presence and participation of all who believed. The rewards and responsibility of a queerly imagined future belonged to everyone.

CONCLUSION

And what sort of future, for us, reflects a queer moral imaginary? I surmise that it will be more than an alteration of perception and a suspension of reality; it will be the result of different social, political, and economic investments. It will be an honest reflection of our confrontation with normative power dynamics, systemic oppression, and unchallenged privilege. It will be about our conversion from limited rule-followers to liberated builders of queer possibilities.

Biblical texts are always sites of politics. They are spaces that contain the negotiation of power and privilege. As an ethicist, I look at biblical texts through the lens of privilege-subversion and with the intent of dismantling that power. That is, I think about what is said directly and/or indirectly within the text that supports the de-stabilization of both current and historic hegemonic notions of power. I am interested in whether or not, or to what degree, the text allows for people who are minoritized, marginalized, erased, ignored, and violated to be centered, acknowledged, valued, and freed from limiting identity constructs and oppressive realities. Even more than the *episteme* (knowledge) regarding human lives, communities, and social relations within the text, I am concerned with the *technē* (method) embedded therein. I want to know what intentional methods, practices, and actions generate such lives, communities, and relations.

Acts 10 serves as a reminder of and response to the technologies that establish personhood, relations, and power soon after Jesus' ascension. Through Peter's words, which mirror Jesus' divine utterances and proclamations in the Sermon on the Mount, Luke proffers a reconstitution of the subject—a recapitulation of persons—within the context of the early church. For Luke, the structures and strictures that ground different identities within the context of a new faith community must be transformed so that members of the community—new believers—can perceive and live into a different kind of future than they had imagined. Imagining new worlds and engaging in transformative agency are, after all, ways of actively responding to the movement of the Holy Spirit.

When I write about the survival and livability and futures of blackness and queerness, I am imagining a new world. I am doing science fiction. I participate in the construction of worlds and social relations that are built on notions of subjectivity that we do not currently possess or with which we do not quite operate. When I talk about the revolutionary quality of black love, I am making a statement about how the reality of black love stands in opposition to the moral discourse that we have used to describe black lives. Between the potential lack of a future due to the expendability of black labor and the socially and religiously sanctioned erasure and demonization of queer sexuality, it makes sense to say that black (queer) lives do not currently matter. Articulation of anything opposite of that is science fiction . . . or moral imagination.

For this reason, a future that insists on blackness and queerness, refuses normativized limitation and resists total destruction and elimination. In such a possible future, the cultivation of difference, rather than the elimination of aberrance, is the aim. Like Luke, I am not interested in a future community governed by the rules of the past, wherein our community's wholeness is built upon precarious boundaries between a demonized other and ourselves. That kind of oversimplified unity is an investment in and justification of collective fragility. Instead, I am looking for a future where rules are broken.

Breaking, or perhaps disabling, a future that is limited by an imagination-less past, does not protect one set of bodies and lives at the expense of others. It is not predicated upon the sacrifice of some for the sake of a few. This dismantling ensures *all* of our livability and is built on the recognized need for protection of *each* body, each life. Consequently, we need to viciously and unapologetically commit to the space-making, system-destroying, norm-releasing work that is required for all of us to live. We ought to do away with both the political and economic structures and the limited visions of relating that are solely built on a denigration of difference. That kind of framework only allows us to know human beings as functional objects, and objects have no future. They have no room to become. Subjects, on the other hand, do have a future. All we need is to own the possibility of our subject transformation and call such change into the here and now.

ROUNDTABLE CONVERSATION

1. Universalism and Particularity

Eric: In your introduction you note, "What the text does NOT do is erase particularity in the service of supporting this notion of nonpartiality. Instead, it shows how universalism, the cultivation of a collective, is still possible with the presence of difference." This strikes me as right, but it also makes me nervous because of the way that "universalism" is typically deployed. Especially I worry that universalism usually entails the flattening of difference. I find myself often feeling allergic to such understandings of universalism because they tend to boil down to accommodation to majority culture. In short, too often "universalism" means, "Let's all be white people." Let's all be like the majority culture. Let's all accommodate the structures of the world as they stand today rather than imagining how God's drawing of peoples together sparks a new imagination for what unity looks like.

Nikki: For me, God's universal acceptance is not akin to a watering down of human creation. Instead, the universality speaks to the universal access that we all have to God's love, grace, forgiveness, and providence. Such a thing doesn't require our sameness; it does, however, point to the very real possibility of our differences in experience, identity, motivation, and circumstance.

Eric: Perhaps then we should think about *why* we—or at least I—don't like terms like "universal" but also "transcendent." What kind of theological thinking and speech helps preserve and lift up particularity and how such particularities are grounded in everyday experiences, not just transcendent space?

Nikki: How does this get lifted by the notions of queerness and queer theology? Moreover, how do we understand Peter's conversion experience through a queer lens? Do we all find that helpful? These are musings that underlie my thought process in the chapter.

Eric: Yes, I think that's most helpful. It may also help us with a related concern I have with "universalism" as it is typically used. In too much of the analysis of early Christianity, Judaism is maligned and caricatured as nationalistic and ethnocentric in sharp contrast to a Christianity that is universal and all-embracing. That contrast is not only historically problematic, it also highlights early Christianity at the expense of our Jewish neighbors. In short, universalism and Christianity are good, while ethnocentrism and Judaism are bad. So, how do we talk about those shifts in experience and encounter without maligning ancient Judaism? How do we address the text in a way that doesn't reaffirm and give sanction to anti-Judaism? One option seems to be to acknowledge that our contexts, our exegetical and theological heritage always carries the danger—perhaps even the certainty—that we will approach or enact an anti-Jewish reading of the text. That is, the weight of our theological and exegetical heritage around anti-Jewish interpretations of this text is so heavy that we will participate in such readings even when we seek to avoid them. Acknowledging that historical weight feels honest, even necessary, but insufficient at the same time. It reminds us of the need to read alongside others, for others can so often note what we cannot see for ourselves.

Jacob: Speaking of the history of interpretation, there's been a tendency (in my context, anyway) to construe Peter's story as the white, straight man's story. Peter is the protagonist, and it will come as no surprise that white, straight men like to be the protagonist in the stories we tell ourselves about ourselves. Your point is crucial, Eric, because it reminds us that we are reading texts coming out of a Jewish context with Gentiles overhearing. We cannot overlook the power-knowledge dynamics at play here: Peter had the power to exclude others. How do people from less dominant/dominating contexts find themselves in this narrative?

Eric: The trick is that even in colonial contexts such power-knowledge dynamics are still at play. For instance, in so much of Latin America, whiteness—as a racial construction—is valorized so that there is not creative room to embrace the richness of the diversity of Latin American racial and ethnic identities.

Jacob: Is this, then, also universal: our tendency to externalize certain features in order to exclude others? It forces me to ask better questions of the text. Who's telling the story? Who is narrating it? How is the Spirit doing work upon these writers and readers and characters?

Eric: Perhaps the posture I might commend is a posture of critique with trust.

Nikki: I want to make pause for a moment to trouble our language of "white straightness" and offer, instead, that we name the dominant perspective of which we are speaking. White straightness is certainly pointing to an identity category, which is important, but we should say that the description houses power, privilege, perspective. . . . That is, we can use that term to denote an entire viewpoint, and if we do so without naming the power embedded within the descriptive phrase, I think we are colluding (at least linguistically) with the process of attributing silent and ongoing power and dominance to white straight men.

And now, back to your conversation: what if prophetic speech is something in which Peter AND I engage in the chapter? Is there some way in the end to say that this kind of speech can fund prophetic speech like the one that I just did in this chapter? Can Peter's speech make possible new speech from readers? Can other people do this, essentially?

2. Creativity and the Divine

Jacob: Let's go back to the title of our book. Is speaking in tongues of mortal and angels a narrative or a divine possibility? Maybe Luke is pointing to an originary creativity, whose queerness is always already stifled by our discursive frames. That is, is it God or us who speaks? Do we possess innate capacities to speak in ways that foster genuine encounter with others, or do we require a divine intervention to snap us out of our epistemological and discursive solipsism?

Nikki: Our creative activity is a reflection of God's image of us, of God's breath enlivening us. In that case, I'm willing to say that it's both. Or, how about this: those two things are not mutually exclusive in my mind. Our participation in creativity is what makes us part of the divine; our creative capacity connects us to God and re-affirms our participation in God's work.

Jacob: In Acts, the Holy Spirit is the star of the show. The Spirit is doing the deconstructive work that we see in Peter's encounter with Cornelius. However, we tend to choose "the Father" in trinitarian language and stress the omni- words whereas what we see in Acts is that the Spirit is the star. The Spirit is unwieldy. The creativity that creates space for our creativity is what ties us to God and that same spirit is doing the deconstructive work we see in Peter's encounter with Cornelius. In the end, it's undecidable. When you preach an amazing sermon, when you feel the spirit at work, it's undecidable how much was me and how much was God, the Spirit interceding.

Nikki: Jacob, who is the "we" in your statement? I'm asking because I wonder if it has an impact on your claim. What if my "we" does not tend to draw heavily on "the Father" or lean into trinitarian language? I'm thinking here of some of my very spiritually grounded sisters who think of the trinity only occasionally, though they deeply appreciate the communal aspect of God's person. Or, I'm thinking of my time in seminary when it was almost anathema to use "Father" or any masculine language when referencing God. Does this change the tenor of your point at all?

Jacob: Thanks for spotting that, Nikki. When I say "we," I'm signifying the position of power that has shaped both my theology and my way of being in the world. Mostly white, mostly straight men have a vested interest in affirming the centrality of the Father and, by extension, shushing the Spirit. In my tradition, God as Father provides the axis around which the world order spins. In contrast, the Spirit scares the hell out of us because there's a shimmy in the axis. And, in my context, when the Spirit is emphasized, it is serving the purpose of offering a theological "hoorah!" to the expansion of the church. The Spirit helps "us" duplicate ourselves. If God is an unchanging, all-powerful entity, then God can ensure "my" position of dominance over others.

Nikki: That makes sense to me. It also makes sense that the term "we" could go totally uninterrogated. And to your point, instead of reading the Spirit as doing some especially different labor, what we see is the Spirit participating in creative activity that would have already been done.

Eric: It strikes me that the questions you are posing, Nikki, are at the heart of the narrative shape of Acts. The Spirit consistently and continually surprises the "we" by noting that the "we" is always bigger or, better, different than the "we" "we" imagined. I hope that makes sense. As I was speaking, I realized I had to trouble both the "We's!"

Nikki: "*We*" get it ;) So, on another note, or maybe back to our early conversation. I want to mention that Peter is not only deconstructing the world, but he is also reimagining what obedience looks like. What you said Jacob is that the notion of a powerful divine entity shifts in that conversation. How? It shifts because we listen to what God says because God is changing, susceptible to our contexts.

Jacob: Let's think about people in my life who insist on the sinfulness of "gay lifestyle." There are many people who wish that there weren't biblical texts that say that these people are "bad" in some way. This might be an interesting way of speaking to that. If God can't change God's mind, then the whole idea that the Spirit might be saying something different to us now is off the table.

3. What Is Old, What Is New

Eric: Let's then think about what Luke is doing in Luke-Acts. He basically is rehearsing old stories in the narrative of Israel. Luke is saying, in a sense, that things are new AND not new. So then, in Acts 10, this feels new to Peter, but Luke has set us up to know that it is not exactly new. It is reminiscent of work that is already being done. God has already set a path and the surprise is less about newness than it is about our ability or capacity to read what is already there. The newness is our capacity to perceive the reality of our creativity. We might call this "traditioned newness" or "traditioned innovation," to use L. Gregory Jones's term.

Nikki: The newness is perceived; after this vision, what "new worlds" are opened up? What we're talking about is a shifting relationship with the divine. We're talking about how the new world deconstructs my human relationships and reconstructs it under the possibility that God can change God's mind and the Spirit is nudging us to participate in it.

Eric: For preachers then the goal in reading and preaching these texts is to help others see themselves as creative agents more than it is about expositing texts or people. Preaching is about plumbing the depths of what these texts and the encounters they narrate make possible.

Nikki: Perhaps then what universalism does is erase the reality of alterity. We are not only talking about difference. We are also taking about temporal, spatial, critical posture. The things that allow us to see differently. This perception is what allows us to live in right relationship with God and one another.

Jacob: Derrida in *The Gift of Death* has a conversation with Levinas about the Akedah. The conversation brings to the fore the undecidability between a response to the divine other and the human other. Derrida thinks Levinas collapses the two: the divine is just the human other. But the divine remains a distinct other but not radically separate of humans: this is a double bind, these competing forces competing for our love.

Nikki: This reminds me of two different songs "The Jesus in Me!" and "I Need You to Survive." Both reflect an insight from Derrida, which suggests that we experience the divine in the eye of the other. I agree with Derrida on this point and would say that God can be found in the human other.

Eric: Yes! We could look in the eye of the other and still see an enemy, but when the divine, that is the Spirit, shows up, something transforms the way that I see the other. We can equip folks to shift what we expect when we encounter the stranger or the other. We can move into joy or expectation rather than fear or doubt.

Jacob: From my denominational context, conversion is viewed as a radical new reality. The symbolic efficacy of baptism is a dying to one's old way of being and rising to participate in the new life inaugurated in and through Jesus. We often assume that Paul's conversion is the emblematic turn in Acts. This can alienate those of us who have "always" been in church and have not had such a radical conversion experience.

Eric: In our thinking about conversion, many of us tend to imagine a conversion of who I think I am, but what if conversion transforms our imagination about who we think our neighbor is?

NOTES

1. Thelathia Nikki Young, *Black Queer Ethics, Family, and Philosophical Imagination* (New York: Palgrave Macmillan, 2016), 196.
2. José Esteban Muñoz, *Disidentifications: Queers of Color and the Performance of Politics* (Minneapolis: University of Minnesota Press, 1999), ix.
3. Ibid., 195.

Chapter Four

Strange Speech: Acts 17:16–34

Eric D. Barreto

Biblical scholars, especially those focused on Acts, seem particularly drawn to the scenes that unfurl around Paul, Athens, and the Areopagus. It's a fascinating story, one that invites so much exegetical consideration. What kind of Athens does Luke imagine? One that represents the heights of philosophical contemplation or a city that has lost its way? What is Paul's approach to Athenian religiosity? Skepticism or accommodation? What is the importance of this narrative to Luke and to us as his modern readers?

As I argued in chapter 1, God's creation is marked by difference: gendered, racialized, embodied. Too often, however, theology has tended to reject particularity and difference as theologians and biblical scholars alike have sought a universal word that can transcend chronologies and localities.[1] In this way, theology could speak to all places and all peoples and all times. Bereft of context, theology is imagined to be free to enlighten anyone, anywhere, anytime. Interpretations of Luke's narration of Paul's encounter with Greek philosophers in Athens are exemplars of such theological assumptions. Here, it was argued, we find a Paul free from all the pesky particularities of culture. Here we find a Paul engaging in the universalizing abstractions of the best of Greek thought. Here we see ourselves as true heirs of the Greek philosophical tradition and thus true heirs of a word that can speak to all people in all places at all times.[2]

Of course, such a reading of the Areopagus scene may have little to do with Lukan theology. And, indeed, a theology set free from cultural "constrictions" is not worthy of its name.

Gender, ethnicity, sexual orientation, and language itself exert tremendous force on how we speak and write theology. Thus, God-talk is a practice of encountering difference and particularity not in an effort to erase either or both. In short, the Areopagus story might spark in us a strange mode of speech for strange times.

A LOCAL SPEECH AT A LOCAL TIME

The narrative of Acts is littered with cultural encounters. From the gathered Judeans speaking various languages at Pentecost to the dramatic embrace of difference embodied in the meeting of Cornelius and Peter, Acts is a narrative of cultural and theological particularity. Local "color" adorns the itineraries of the missionaries of Acts. Identity and its contestation are thus central to the narrative of Acts. Critical to understanding these negotiations is the post-colonial notion of hybridity, a powerful though subtle form of identity and resistance in colonial contexts. In this way, Acts provides a critical starting point, an imaginative spark for wondering how we might speak of theology in the midst of contested epistemologies and identities. Theology in such contexts emerges not from universal categories applicable in many times and place but in the kind of embodied, enculturated encounters narrated in the Book of Acts.

Paul's proclamation in Athens has attracted a great deal of scholarly attention from a guild and a culture that traces its intellectual roots back to the philosophical schools of Athens and Greece. As a symbolic cultural progenitor, Athens is an important site. It is little surprise then that scholars find in Paul's presentation of the gospel to the Athenians the encounter par excellence of the religious and philosophical traditions most central to the study of the New Testament.

Scholars have tended to emphasize the universal dimensions of Paul's proclamation at Athens, arguing that Luke's Paul here engages in a philosophical discourse designed to encompass and persuade all peoples. By this, some seem to assume that the distinctly Greek setting of Paul's speech marks it as universal. There is a sense in the scholarship that this sermon could have been preached anywhere in the Gentile world. The contrary is true. This is a scene and speech fine-tuned to the narratively constructed ethos and particularities of an Athens holding on to an ancient legacy of philosophical sophistication but now experiencing a gradual but inexorable fall into insatiable but unavailing curiosity.[3] While Greek heritage is a cultural touchstone for much of Western culture, Paul's encounter with Greece does not necessarily mark it as a foundational moment in the narrative of Acts. In contrast, I contend that this scene is far more local than it is universal. The events of Acts 17:16–34 are more particular to the Athenian ethos constructed by Luke than they are transcendent of individual cultures and thus applicable to all.

And so my reading of the Areopagus scene boils down to two observations. First, Luke's narration of the Areopagus events is yet another instantiation of his careful orchestration of vibrantly local scenes. That is, Luke highlights the unique features of Athens in order to emphasize this particular setting. Paul's proclamation here is tailored to the peculiar character of Athens, not the wider world. Second, Paul's sermon trades on notions of ethnicity.[4] The broader proclamation present at the Areopagus is in the Lukan Paul's strategic deployment of ethnic discourse. In other words, Paul's speech deals directly with the proliferation of ethnic difference and how the endurance of ethnic difference is an integral component of God's working among the nations. Thus, the encounter of Athenian curiosity and Pauline proclamation is yet another instance of Luke's negotiation of the wide claims of the gospel in the diverse and particular communities of the ancient world.

A full exegetical detailing of these conclusions would take much more space than I have.[5] But, more importantly, this reading of the Areopagus is not the end of our argument but a critical means to it. The history of interpretation of this text reveals a critical problem in theological discourse. By conjoining universality, transcendence, and Greek philosophical thought or at least its imprimatur, we have too easily sought to elide difference, particularity, and place; in this way, we have tended to demean their importance in the construction of theology.

In short, the scene in Areopagus stands as a representative sample of the theological negotiations around difference Luke constructs. When the good news arrives in the diverse locales of the Mediterranean world, the gospel finds root in rich local soil. That is, the good news is always *particular*, not *universal* in its instantiations. However, in its particularity and rootedness in a particular place and among a particular people, the narrating of these local events is nonetheless relevant to the reader of Acts, no matter who she is. In the end, Luke is drawing local portraits of the gospel finding root meant to inspire believers to root themselves wherever they are.

Initially, let's remind ourselves of this narrative. In Acts 17:16, Paul finds himself in Athens awaiting the arrival of his travel companions. As he does elsewhere in Acts, Paul begins contending for the gospel in synagogues as well as in the marketplace. He particularly draws the attention of two kinds of philosophers, Epicureans and Stoics. Their interactions with Paul, however, seem marked by confusion; they either dismiss him or misunderstand him (see v. 18). So, they bring Paul to the Areopagus to learn more about this strange proclamation Paul is bringing to Athens. Parenthetically, Luke whispers in v. 21 that the residents of Athens had taken to chasing after whatever new idea they could find. Paul thus begins his famous speech. He begins by (perhaps) praising his hearers, noting their religious devotion as evidenced by the presence of so many shrines. Among these many "objects of worship," he reports finding a shrine "to an unknown God." That God, Paul says is whom I bring to you. He subtly critiques idolatry, evokes the story of Adam without naming him explicitly, and quotes local poets. The speech ends when Paul evokes the resurrection, at which point some scoff but a few believe.

A few highlights then from the exegesis of this passage: first is to notice the distress which marks Paul's reaction to the redolent idolatry of Athens. This is a city marked not by philosophical inquiry from Luke's perspective but by an unanchored intellectual curiosity and religious inquisitiveness (see v. 21). This is a city, though once great, that has fallen on hard times, intellectually speaking. And so, when some Athenian locals tag Paul as a *spermologos*, there is a narrative irony present. After all, Paul is not the intellectual scavenger who indiscriminately picks up bits of knowledge here and there. That the Athenians have even erected a statue to an unknown God is both a sign of their intellectual and religious decline but also a mark of their need for Paul's proclamation from Luke's perspective.

Indeed, Paul's proclamation in Athens is both accommodating and critical. It is hybrid in its form and message. Most accommodating may be the absence of the name of Jesus in Paul's speech. Instead, Paul tells the story of "a man whom [God] has appointed," a story that interweaves the idolatry that Luke's Paul finds so infuriating and the stirring words of local poets. The story Paul tells is both Athenian and Jewish at one and the same time. If the reader knows the stories of the Hebrew Scriptures, the sketch Paul draws of the history of God and God's people is discernible. But so too is it discernible to the Athenians, who presumably do not see themselves in the story of Israel. Some embrace this story. Some are intrigued. Some are dismissive. The various receptions have to do not with Paul's clarity but with the receptivity of those hearing the message.

Key to Luke's ethnic argumentation is v. 26. Basically, Luke argues that a single common source links every *ethnos*. This is not a confession of cultural homogeneity, that all *ethnē* are basically the same because they share one common ancestry. Neither is mere universality in view here. Instead, the link here is between one and every. A single cultural ancestor paradoxically explains our differences. Our differences are bound up in the one progenitor of all peoples. Such an understanding of the beginning of v. 26 then brings clarity to the admittedly complex phrasing that closes Paul's speech. Specifically, what do we make of the cryptic reference to "seasons and boundaries" in v. 26? We ought to be careful in interpretation not to import subtly colonial notions of nationhood and peoples. Luke does not have in mind the boundaries cartographers and empires draw between us nor simply the historical narratives the powerful construct to explain their ascendancy. The clearest referent of this admittedly complex phrase is perhaps rather simple. The world is big and diverse, populated by a wide variety of peoples and cultures. We are not all the same though our origin is unitary. That is, we are linked by a common origin from "one" but distinguished by God's own hand, which is precisely why this speech is aimed at these Athenians and not on a universal stage of generic humans.

But let's return to the opening of v. 26. As the source of all, God's primordial role in the dispersion of the peoples of the world is entirely consequential. How exactly Paul expresses this is a source of scholarly debate. There is not an explicit referent provided for the adjective *enos* (one). Not surprisingly, textual critical evidence suggests that later manuscripts sought to clarify the indefinite referent of *enos*, most by supplying *haimatos* (blood), perhaps suggesting that from early on in the manuscript tradition ethnic discourses were underwriting interpretation. Text critical criteria rather definitively conclude that nouns attached to *enos* were later additions. I would add an internal reason to buttress the manuscript evidence. Without a scribal addendum, the wordplay between *enos* and *ethnos* comes to the forefront; that is from *enos* came every *ethnos*. A further word play or at least semantic link is then also evident in v. 27 when Paul concludes that God is indeed not far from any one (*enos*) of us. Any individual is therefore always linked to all others thanks to a common ancestry but also the persistent bonds of culture, kinship, and ethnicity.

At this point, however, we ought to move carefully. The theological point in view here remains the creation of all by God, so the "one" is the primordial human, from whom descended all the peoples of the world. In other words, it is God's hand that multiplies the peoples, cultures, and religions of the world but also God's creative acts that undergirds a broad scope to the church's mission, making possible the proclamation of the good news in Athens, Jerusalem, and Rome alike. It is too common for interpreters today to conclude that this means the erasure of difference, the transcendence of all that makes us particular. As Tannehill writes, "The necessary resources [to preach a universal message] are found through reflection on the relation the Creator to the creation. This is a relation that transcends every ethnic and racial difference."[6] By means of the creation, the argument follows, foreignness is eradicated in our relationship to God and one another, for all peoples have a common ancestry rooted in God's originating act.

This is a misreading of Athens but more importantly of the theology of Acts. Remember it is the particularity of Athens, its distinctive cultural features that become a means by which Paul can share the good news. The Athenians are still Athenians. The Judeans are still Judeans. The Romans are still Romans. The "seasons and boundaries" remain in place even as the gospel calls for all peoples to follow the way God has set.

If Paul is right, then what does devotion to God look like in the pluralistic religious milieu of Athens? That is the question lingering in the air as Paul continues this missionary sermon. The final quotation of v. 28 provides the crucial link as he draws out the theological implications of being one of God's children: "Because we are offspring of God." The inclusion of the full span of humanity within God's family is a radical step and relies on the doctrine of God's creation of all from one. As Johnson argues, "Here truly is a fundamental step, an affirmation of human culture not as sufficient in itself, but as a worthy vehicle for the truth of the gospel toward which, unwittingly, it was striving."[7]

Local particularity is therefore key. This is not a neutral scene set at the crossroads of the Greek philosophical tradition. Instead, we have a city with a mixed heritage. Though once the pinnacle of philosophical contemplation, Athens is now a collection of pseudo-philosophers seeking something new to discuss. In their search for something new, idols have overgrown the city. In this way, Luke draws a complex critique of a once great city. The pretensions of this movement of followers of Jesus are lofty, striving to be heard and embraced even in this most learned city. But the proclamation of the gospel also lays bare the folly of this new Athens, a city now characterized by an un-availing search for something innovative. In short, this narrative is not characterized by tepid tolerance or unwavering rejection. Something more subtle is at work as Acts negotiates a discursive space for a faith that embraces the particularities that characterize the peoples of the world.

Ultimately, then the portrait of Athens in Acts 17 is conducted in a hybrid tone, in a multivalent tone, in a harmonious while also dissonant tone. On the one hand, the heights of Athenian philosophical achievements underwrite the legacy of the city. Equally, however, it is the evident crumbling of this philosophical edifice that provides the Paul of Acts space to make a bold claim that these Christ followers are taking up the mantle of Athens's former greatness. At core, Acts 17 bridges the particular, local color of the narrated Athens and a proclamation that calls all peoples to repent. That proclamation rests on the very presence of our differences; it does not call for those differences to cease to be. Human difference then is the very essence, the ideal medium for the proclamation of the good news.

CONCLUSION

Because of the story's setting in Athens and Western affinities for the philosophical traditions symbolized by that city, the Areopagus scene has taken on oversized significance in the scholarship of Acts. Specifically, a vast swath of the scholarship has contended that Luke's setting of this story in Athens, a center of such culture-transcending philosophical importance, means that the significance of this narrative is universal. It transcends a particular time and place precisely through the means of the city's philosophical heights. And so, this story becomes an emblem of all kinds of intercultural and cross-cultural encounters. It becomes a guides for missionary encounters and cultural cross-roads. It becomes a guide for God-talk that crosses the boundaries language, culture, and place erect. Indeed, Paul's appeal to the creation of all through "one man," means that this is a universal story, relevant no matter which cultural space from which someone might be reading.

But what if the speech and scene in Athens is far stranger, far more particular than it is universal? Paul's Areopagus speech to the people in Athens is not a flattening of cultural difference but an expression in honor of difference. In fact, Paul leans into a certain bilingualism and biculturalism that helps us think about a way of speaking of God that embraces the strangeness of speech, a strangeness always already at work in speech. The implications for how we speak of God in these strange languages are manifold but especially the insight that all such talk of God is rooted in a particular place and time, whether in ancient Athens or elsewhere in our modern world.

1. God-talk will always be strange to someone, familiar to another.

Because theology is always rooted in a place, time, and culture, its commitments will resonate among some and seem strange to others. This is not a bug in theological discourse; it is its very essence. Perhaps then our ears ought to be attuned to that God-talk that resonates with our experiences but also that which sounds jarring, unexpected, strange. Indeed, even if God-talk is in a language we know and spoken by someone who shares cultural space with us, we should expect such theology to be strange to us. After all, none of us fully inhabits the cultural space another inhabits.

Of course, such strangeness can find a source in cultural particularity as much as it can in misshaped theology. Theology can sound strange to us because it has misunderstood who God is or who God's creatures are. Theology can be rooted in flawed, broken assumptions as much as it can in the rich soil of God's diverse cultures. So, there's an additional layer of complexity at play. Such strange speech asks for discernment in communities of belonging. In such communities, we can (imperfectly) suss out what is theological from what lacks truth. The distinction, therefore, is not between what is theological and cultural as so many of us have been taught. We have been told to find the theological core of an argument or a doctrine or a piece of Scripture, separating what is truthful from what is cultural or particular. In the study of Scripture, we have been taught to separate exegesis (drawing out from the texts its meaning) from eisegesis (adding meanings that the text does not itself hold). But what if that distinction is less than helpful or truthful? What if the distinction we need to draw is between strange theologies that shape us as God's creatures and other still strange theologies that misshape us?

2. Clarity in our speaking about God and one another will not emerge in translation as much as in encounter.

But how can we tell the difference between true theology and misshapen theology? The imagination sparked by the Areopagus scene suggests that such clarity will emerge not in translation as much as in encounter. It will not prove sufficient to put the theological insights of one cultural space and time into new words and in new contexts. Instead, we must encounter such strange speech in all its particularity.

There are limits of course to this kind of encounter. None of us can fully inhabit the linguistic and cultural spaces of another contemporary let alone those of the ancient communities that produced and first received these texts. But what if translation is not the end of our theological inquiry but the means by which we can encounter strange speech?

Such is one of the gifts of teaching Greek to seminarians. Many of my students enter my classroom excited finally to unlock the mysteries of Scripture. The implicit assumption is that knowing the ancient languages will clarify and demystify, that syntax and grammar and vocabulary can make clear passages that had previously befuddled them. To be sure, Greek is a valuable tool in the study of the New Testament but perhaps not the tool such students initially expect to pick up. Learning Greek is not akin to picking up a shovel. That is, the meaning of these texts is not hidden underneath the words, so to speak. Greek is not a shovel by which we can dig and pile up all that obstructs what we might find in these texts. Instead, Greek tends to make these ancient texts that much stranger. The syntax of the language remains strange even after years of study. The scope of a word's definition remains still twisted up in a jumble of other words and ancient experiences. Greek does not give us a shovel by which we can get past the particularities of place and time and culture; it's a means by which we enter this strange, sometimes confusing space.

3. Clarity in our speaking about God and one another will not emerge in discerning a universal connection among various, strange ways of speaking but in encountering strange people in the strange places and strange times in which they speak.

If we encounter texts with roots in a strange place and time, then how do we read them? The dominant reading of the Areopagus has suggested that philosophy or some other form of abstraction can help us bridge the cultural gap between then and now, between us and them. Some universal insight can link us across time and space. But the reading I've suggested above might lead us to a stranger, yet more insightful, space.

Perhaps we could think about it in this way. What if we see ourselves as curious guests in someone else's narration of God's activity in a particular place and time? Our aim as curious guests is to listen, observe, ask questions, but we never take ownership over what we hear. We can never become hosts of such cultural spaces; we remain but appreciative guests. And thus we encounter this strange talk about God and imagine how this encounter might return us back home changed. That is, we don't leave these encounters with a kernel of insight that can be planted in just any soil. Instead, we encounter the stories about God that others have told, and in that encounter we find our imaginations about who God might be and what God might do clarified and expanded beyond the, yes, rich but also constricted spaces that have shaped us.

4. Those who wish to proclaim this strange but blessed news must seek deep roots along with a willingness to travel.

The implications for preachers and teachers, those who would like to say something about God and God's creation, are striking to me. We must come to know the places that have shaped us, the cultures that have given us a sense of self and community and other. There is much richness in this kind of exploration, for God's creative touch can be discerned in the multiplicity and particularity of our cultures. There is, of course, a great deal of bias, prejudice, brokenness, and misshapen assumptions to be discerned as well. Such a search can be equally fruitful, liberating us from narrow narratives we have inherited about who God is and what God might do.

But the Areopagus scene also suggests that staying in one place just won't do. We have to be willing to take the risk to travel, to leave those cultural spaces that shape us but sometimes confine us and our imaginations. Indeed, much of the narrative of Acts takes place on the roads Rome built and the cities these roads connected. The strangeness of Athens and Ephesus and

Eric D. Barreto

Philippi alike helps form the narrative of Acts and thus our understanding and embodying of the gospel. We ought not resolve that strangeness, domesticating any of these places for the sake of a universal theological thread which anyone can grasp. Instead, Athens opens up the gospel to a people who would not have heard it otherwise.

And in Luke's narration of that encounter, we too learn something. We don't learn that the Athenian philosophical tradition can carry the weight of the gospel to all people and places. No, we learn that this city, its mix of achievement and deep flaws, is a home God chooses for the gospel. And that is true of the other cities the protagonists of Acts visit. And it's true of the spaces we dwell today.

ROUNDTABLE CONVERSATION

1. Points of View and Roots of Speech

Jacob: Eric, there's some really great stuff here! What you are describing will be incredibly helpful for students and congregations to think about who they understand themselves to be in relation to others. The work of philosopher José Medina can help us here. In his book *Speaking from Elsewhere*, Medina differentiates between two primary modes of discourse. The dominant mode, which underwrites the traditional reading of this pericope that you challenge, is the view from *nowhere.* This is a universalizing and normative mode of speaking that flattens cultural particularities. By contrast, the view from *here,* captured so well by standpoint theorists, stresses cultural particularity. It maintains that where one stands ineluctably shapes how one sees the world and makes meaning out of it. Medina then offers a third way: a view from *else*where. Here he affirms the insights about the importance of recognizing one's cultural particularities from standpoint theorists, but he also wants to move us to ways of speaking across difference. His work allows us to value our points of overlap and move us toward mutual recognition.

Nikki: The idea that Luke is arguing for a common source is really important to notice, and Eric does a good job of highlighting this. There *is* something to be said about what we do share. In my estimation, the reason we think and talk about diversity is not because we hail from the same space. (For me this is key, because Luke is not calling for some unnamed normative ethic. That is, he is not ushering us toward an ethic that emerges from narratives or religious and social scripts that establish norms.) We talk about diversity because we come from different locations, motivations, investments, experiences, constructs, etc. Eric deals with the text in a way that illustrates how we are all leaning into a mode of being with God that, in turn, structures our relations to one another and conditions our seeing. Again, a unitary origin is less important than an ethic of relation that draws us to attend to diversity and particularity.

Eric: In his speech, Paul is talking about Adam without naming the character in Genesis 2 overtly. It's less an ethic that binds us together than a story that gives us an ethic.

Nikki: Nice! Well, there is something good about narrative coherence, since it helps us notice and acknowledge a common aim (Alasdair MacIntyre).

Eric: But now I'm wondering about something else. In the West, we tend to function within an epistemology that yearns for coherence. Western thought seems to lean towards wanting things to hold together, to mitigate contradictions, and to resolve tensions. But what if the Athens narrative drives us toward a different imagination. That is, do the cacophony of stories and voices present in the scene in Athens point to a desire for coherence but also to the reality of diverse stories and experiences?

Nikki: The stories allow us to actually perceive one another. This is central to your ethnic argument, Eric. Even more, what jumps out for me is that the simultaneity of social or ethnic constructs and the universality of God's creativity are necessary.

Jacob: The fact that prototypical biblical scholars identify with Paul as protagonist or speaker maps onto the particular, especially of white straight men. We see ourselves. Therefore, the elision masks the violent suppression and rejection of difference. What does it mean to have Paul as a white- or man-splainer? Instead, Eric is saying that Luke is doing something different.

In fact, Eric's discussion made me think of Deleuze and Guatarri in *A Thousand Plateaus*, especially in relation to the idea of a root that is unified and manifesting in different spaces. They associate this with a rhizome. A better image, and one so abundant in my Georgia context, is kudzu: it is both skirting over the top of the ground and taking root in different spaces. The notion of root in this paragraph might be working against what you are trying to say here, Eric, especially since root identity is based on a mythical past, as opposed to relational identity, which is archipelagogical, a relation between these languages, peoples, and practices (Glissant).

Eric: It's helpful to test the metaphors we employ. You're right that roots might imply something static, something that holds on to a particular piece of ground. Here, I want to imagine this root language being about the reality that we are always somewhere. Root language is about "being in a place." And yet, our roots are movable; we can be planted elsewhere. In short, roots don't fix us to a place for all time; roots place us in a context. Seeing the complexity of this image, I think calls us to speech that engages difference.

Jacob: Eric, I wonder about how your particular identity might help us to understand what you are naming in your reading of this pericope. Can you speak to how your Puerto Rican identity has shaped your ways of thinking and speaking?

Eric: Yes, I was born in Puerto Rico, which is both a part of but also apart from the United States. I was born with citizenship, but my identity was named by the culture of the island. But then I moved, like an increasing number of Puerto Ricans. I'm still Puerto Rican though my "roots" are now in New Jersey. When I go back to Puerto Rico, I feel the tension once again of being a part of a place but also apart. Fernando Segovia has called this "living on the hyphen" between Hispanic and American in Hispanic-American. One is both at home and a stranger on both sides of the hyphen.

Nikki: I'm thinking also about the connection between roots and movement. The realities of the Middle Passage and subsequent diaspora provide good examples of a people sharing a collective experience of identity in or with a place that is separate from their location. When I think of my African roots, I am thinking in terms of connections that transcend immediacy and specificity. And they have to, right? The violence of the Trans-Atlantic Slave Trade, which is as much about eviscerating one's connection to "home" as it is about converting humans into things, means that my notion of roots must mean something different that "a place from which I come" or even "a people with whom I belong." Now, the notion of roots is more elastic and shows types of connections that are bound up in narratives, affinities, appreciations, and more. When I identify (in some contexts) as "African American," I am dancing in a world that is at the same unique and nebulous. I distinguish myself as an American *citizen* with African ancestry, but such ancestry bears no particular meaning.

2. Ethnic Notions

Nikki: What is ethnicity? How does it operate in the chapter? Full disclosure, I think it's different from race. It speaks to choices and externally acknowledged affinities to a mythical past and a presumption of a commitment to said past.

Eric: The distinction between race and ethnicity is huge! Full disclosure, I use "race" and "ethnicity" largely synonymously, but that's a rabbit hole we can pursue elsewhere! Let's focus on ethnicity then. I'm saying at least two things about ethnicity. First, in the ways that we talk about ethnicity, we assume that ethnicity is inherited, biological, something we receive. But, second, I see in ethnicity a set of constructed practices and narratives. In practice, ethnicity is flexible, mutable; it is something that we are constantly constructing and reconstructing. Or another way I've come to think about ethnicity is that ethnicity is composed of narratives of belonging that shape how we relate to others.

Nikki: After reading this chapter, I wondered if you think that ethnicity something that is externally described or internally understood. It seems like you're saying that ethnicity is a social construct on one hand, yet it seems to be a part of God's diversity, on the other. Is this problematic or liberating? Is an ethnic identity something we are taking on as divine inheritance or as census material?

Eric: I want to argue that both external description and internal understanding are at play. In some way, it's more a matter of an inheritance, something externally described, even imposed. For example, no "Hispanics" decided to call themselves "Hispanic." The term or category was imposed as a construction, and yet now it has become a source of political power, a way for a wide swath of peoples to claim political voice in a system too often hostile to our needs. It's also internal too, however, in that ethnic identity is constructed as stories we tell ourselves about who we are and where we belong. Such stories require real work. We have to sustain our ethnic identities actively, all the time; we are always performing our identities. I do wonder if this is something communities of color can know a bit more clearly that folks in dominant communities.

Nikki: Can census data become the point from which we speak of God's diversity? Have we gotten it backwards? Does God create ethnic particularity, or do we create it? I have my own opinions, but I want to know what you think, given your reading of the text.

Eric: Can we say that census data is but an index of the complex stories that make up our communities? Such data is a measure but not a story. In Acts, I think Luke is building a narrative wherein God is the author of our differences. Perhaps that theological insight can encounter the sociological insight about the constructedness of ethnicity. For instance, can I think of Puerto Rican identity that doesn't erase the black, brown, and white people that narrated those stories? Plus, how do I grapple with the broken stories that are part of this identity, especially the ways whiteness is valorized in so much of Latin America?

Jacob: If I may add to and further complicate this conversation, let's go back to something you, Eric, just mentioned about the work that ethnic identity requires, particularly for those who are a part of dominant and dominating communities. Can I think of my Caucasian identity apart from the sordid history and continuing effects of white supremacy? It has been a long journey for me to understand my whiteness apart from uncritical valorization or radical denigration. The legacy of whiteness demands repentance and remuneration, and knowing this structures much of my scholarship, teaching, and preaching. I confess that I struggle to appreciate my whiteness, while all the while I benefit from that same whiteness.

Nikki: Part of the way that "we" often talk about ethnic identity is through a lens of pride. I hear it in what both of you are saying. And for some folks, that pride is the foundation of the identity itself. Yet, our pride is not an inherent thing. As you mention, Eric, we are told how to count heritage (based on colonialism, the formation of nation states, neoliberalism, etc.), but somehow that does not negate our ethnic identity. Pride of ethnicity does not have to be linked with a story of loss and oppression, or embarrassment and guilt. Or does it?

Eric: Yes, I think this speaks to the question of diversity in churches, too. There is also some messed up stuff in all of our communities. Our stories about identity are just as in need of transformation and "good news" as any part of our lives. But, and this is key, the solution is not the resolving of all our stories into a single story but diverse stories that encounter one another with grace and curiosity.

Nikki: How do we seek a liberative discourse that is not centered on the structures of ethnic relations that we inherit from the mouth (and force) of the oppressor?

3. Inclusivity and Divine Community

Jacob: I have a question that comes from early pages in the chapter. You say, "If Paul is right . . . what does devotion look like . . . in Athens?" I thought of John Hick's notion of anonymous Christians. When Paul tries to cast a big inclusive narrative, it silences particular identities that might not want to be included. I am wondering about the degree to which we say, "Yes, this is a model for how we should be thinking about moving forward." For example, in one of his comedy specials, Trevor Noah imagines an encounter between the first Englishmen to arrive in India and an Indian farmer. The Englishman declares to the Indian man, "Congratulations, you are now part of the British Empire." Noah narrates the Indian man's incredulity about being forced to join a group that he'd never heard about. Is Paul doing the same thing to these Athenians? Critiques of Hick might be a way to push back against silencing the full history of inclusion and complexity in the community.

Eric: Paul is going into *a* space to tell a story about *that* place. This is an Athenian sermon through and through, not a universal one. It can't speak to the diverse milieu beyond the boundaries of Athens. Though what you may be cautioning, Jacob, is that the speech may not even be able to speak the diverse milieu of Athens itself! Perhaps Luke's narration of Athens itself has already flattened the city into a province of erstwhile philosophers who have lost their way. There must have been other kinds of people there. And maybe Luke even notes this when he points to those who believed the good news.

Nikki: Sure, but what does it mean to impose meaning onto a community in a way that they might not (immediately) identify? It feels like anthropological signifying.

On a different note, I love the line regarding the strangeness of our language. You mention, Eric, that our language will always be strange to someone, which I think is a beautifully complex thought. I would have loved to hear more about that. I suppose I'm interested because, for me, it's about encounter rather than translation. We try to translate God-talk into our (academic) discourse. Yet, I would rather know about what kind of encounters are made possible in the process of recognizing the strangeness in our language. Jacob, think about how preachers do this. What we want them to do is to fully engage texts and peoples beyond translation.

Jacob: Translation is a big part of most homiletical training, Nikki. It is the obvious next step from the hermeneutical techniques that we teach our students in Bible classes. The challenge—nay, impossibility—of preaching is to structure a space of hospitality for the otherness of the text that works to provide for the text's flourishing in this new context. Just as there is a necessary hostility hardwired to every act of hospitality (i.e., one can never be hospitable *enough*), the practices of sermon development and delivery can be hostile to full engagement. I say a lot more about this in my book *Preaching Must Die! Troubling Homiletical Theology* (Fortress Press, 2017).

Eric: I want to drive towards engagement too, Nikki. To me, what's exciting about engagement is that we can't see the edge of its possibilities. The shape of engagement depends on who is gathered together reading Scripture and speaking about God. So, I want my students in Bible courses to allow Scripture to be a path by which imagination flourishes and possibilities expand. Scripture does not script what those engagements might be but helps create the possibilities of their occurring.

Nikki: The processes that you both describe make me feel good about the cultivation of a divine community. Part of what I hear is that the purpose of the process is to foster an encounter that draws out and perhaps destabilizes one's own interpretive agency and also makes room for others to do the same. This, to me, is the space of possibility and relational flourishing. When the text opens us up to such a process, we are called individually and collectively to be our best selves.

NOTES

1. Nikki Young helped me realize how broad such assumptions are in theology but also how broad its implications are. Theologians have tended to attach notions of wholeness to ideas about universality and unity. That is, as she explained, "Unity parallels wholeness as the power way for individuals and communities to exist. Think, then, about the implications this has for differently abled people or differently-bodied folks."

2. For example, Joseph A. Fitzmyer, *The Acts of the Apostles* (AB 31; New York: Doubleday, 1998), 600, calls this narrative "the most important episode in Pauline Mission II, the evangelization of what had been the most renowned city in ancient Greece." Or as Philipp Vielhauer observes in "On the 'Paulinism' of Acts," in *Studies in Luke-Acts*, ed. L. E. Keck and J. L. Martyn (Mifflintown, PA: Sigler Press, 1980), 34, "At the high point of his book Luke lets Paul make a speech at the Areopagus in Athens before Stoic and Epicurean philosophers, the only sermon to Gentiles by the missionary to the Gentiles to be found in Acts." So also C. K. Barrett, *Acts: A Shorter Commentary* (New York: T&T Clark, 2002), 265, notes, "The speech is . . . a summary of the kind of address to Gentiles that Hellenistic Christians had inherited

Eric D. Barreto

from Hellenistic Jews." He continues, "Christianity was to spend time in a world that had an important intellectual element and that it was necessary that Christians should be able and willing to converse with those who represented this element" (266). A final example is Hans Conzelmann, "The Address of Paul on the Areopagus," in *Studies in Luke-Acts*, ed. L. E. Keck and J. L. Martyn (Mifflintown, PA: Sigler Press, 1980), 217, who calls the speech "the most momentous Christian document from the beginnings of that extraordinary confrontation between Christianity and philosophy." Mark D. Given, "Not Either/or but Both/and in Paul's Areopagus Speech, " *BibInt* 3 (1995): 363, wrote about the speech, "As readers we are about to enter into what is arguably the most sophisticated speech composed by the most accomplished narrator and speech writer in the New Testament."

3. It's important to note that this is *Luke's* narrative construction of Athens. See below.

4. For further development of the significance and meaning of this term, see Eric D. Barreto, *Ethnic Negotiations: The Function of Race and Ethnicity in Acts 16* (Tübingen: Mohr Siebeck, 2010), 27–59.

5. See Eric D. Barreto, *A People for God's Name* (forthcoming).

6. Robert Tannehill, *The Narrative Unity of Luke-Acts: A Literary Interpretation* (Minneapolis: Fortress, 1986–1990), 2:211.

7. Luke Timothy Johnson, *The Acts of the Apostles* (SP 5; Collegeville, MN: The Liturgical Press, 1992), 320.

Chapter Five

Baptismal Speech: Acts 18:24–19:8

Jacob D. Myers

We are born into modes of thinking that precede our being. Our very possibility of thought conforms to patterns established in advance of our speaking. Such patterns we call language.[1] Languages structure our capacity for everyday speech—God-talk included. Apart from language, as the eminent Swiss linguist Ferdinand de Saussure once noted, thought itself is impossible. He writes, "In itself, thought is like a swirling cloud, where no shape is intrinsically determinate. No ideas are established in advance, and nothing is distinct, before the introduction of linguistic structure."[2] How a given culture works to wrangle this proto-linguistic cloud determines every post-linguistic possibility. To put it differently, in language we are not so much able to bend the cloud to our will; we merely learn to live in the cloud in culturally determined ways.

Against this epistemological backdrop, I want to suggest that *baptismal speech* inaugurates new possibilities of thinking and speaking. Much as one may discern a Scottish, Ghanaian, or Bostonian accent on the tongue of a stranger, the nuances of one's grammar and inflection reveal a speaker's origin. But baptismal speech does more; it also heralds one's destination. This, I argue, is its greatest difference from a given parlance. Baptismal speech has the capacity to deliver the speaker into alternative epistemological frames than those pre-coded by her language system. Baptismal speech is always headed somewhere—without necessarily being teleological.[3]

In Acts 18:24–19:8, we encounter three modes of baptismal speech that illuminate contemporary Christian discourse in and beyond ecclesial contexts. The first mode of baptismal speech I label *eloquent speech*. This we may discern on the lips of a certain Apollos. I wish to define eloquent speech as that which masters dominant ways of thinking and speaking. The second discursive paradigm I label *nuanced speech.* Such speech neither capitulates to nor transcends the reigning discursive structures but subverts said structures by participating in them in shrewd ways. This type of baptismal speech tends to manifest on the tongues of oppressed and marginalized persons such as Aquila and Priscilla, Paul's "co-laborers" in Ephesus. The third mode of baptismal speech manifests from a coterie of unnamed "disciples" whom Paul encounters in the Grecian interior regions on his arrival from Corinth. Such I label *prophetic speech.* Prophetic speech transcends discursive norms and ways of thinking. Such "speaking in tongues" receives from God an alternative field of linguistic possibilities. This discourse is indicative of the Holy Spirit's agency.

If America is in the midst of a Fourth Great Awakening, as Diana Butler Bass insists,[4] then we who speak in and beyond ecclesial contexts require new grammars and new vocabularies to participate in the work of God in the world. We need folks who have mastered dominant ecclesial and sociopolitical discourses and who can speak to others from within these discursive frames. We need folks who can give voice to the realities of empire and who are willing to subvert dominant ways of thinking, speaking, and behaving by speaking from those experiences to challenge oppression and marginalization. And we need people to speak in the tongues of angels, those equipped and emboldened by the Spirit to speak new realities into existence.

LUKE'S DISCURSIVE TRAVELOGUE

The second volume of Luke's "orderly account" (ἀκριβῶς καθεξῆς, Lk. 1:3) of Jesus' ministry and the Way that emerged in the wake of Jesus' resurrection reads like a travelogue. It is *topological* as much as it is *tropological*; place matters as much as (or more than) the narrative-historical conventions Luke employs. Luke is especially keen to alert us to the whence and where of his characters. He wants us to know, for instance, that Apollos comes from Alexandria, and that Priscilla and Aquila were kicked out of Rome by imperial edict (18:2), and that Paul encounters these twelve or so "disciples" as he's traveling through the Grecian hinterlands. Luke's narrative/historical specificity highlights how one's geo-political positioning shapes one's baptismal dialect. More on this later.

Even as his narrative trajectory recounts (or announces) the spread of the Jesus-movement from its genesis in Judea to the ends of the earth, *how* Luke tells this story reflects an epistemological ambivalence that must be highlighted as we attend to the three modes of baptismal speech on display in Acts 18:24–19:8. For starters, there is no denying that the Roman *imperium* shapes Luke's worldview.[5] To this point, in their essay "Script(ur)ing Gender in Acts," Penner and Vander Stichele are right to note that the Book of Acts is replete with "images of potent male power brokers dotting (and darting across) the Lukan landscape, being marked also as resistant colonial subjects who proffer a new royal ideology." At the same time, they observe that Luke's characters "both challenge the current configurations of power but in that same moment also reify those same structures by valuing dynamics and aspiring to the aims of *imperium* itself."[6] From a different perspective, Tat-siong Benny Liew directs our attention to Luke's "ethnic monopoly," a sort of "glass ceiling for Gentiles," in Acts in which Jewish "major" (e.g., Peter, John, Paul, Philip) and "minor" (e.g., Apollos, Priscilla, and Aquila) actors receive the credit for advancing the Way, as if the Gentile faithful were altogether absent. Liew is right to remind us that Act's goal is "religious monopoly rather than diversity."[7] Accordingly, we must remember that Luke's narration is shaded by sociocultural, linguistic particularities, and theological aims complexly situated in and beyond imperial consciousness.

As we consider the modes of baptismal speech emerging from Luke's characters, moreover, it is important to underscore the fact that Luke does not convey the particular and peculiar patois of these speakers. This is especially strange when we consider the detailed speeches Luke has recounted thus far. Following the outpouring of the Holy Spirit at Pentecost, we receive Peter's inaugural sermon verbatim in Acts 2. In Acts 3 and 4, Luke spares no space in recounting Peter's speeches at Solomon's Porch and before the Sanhedrin. For fifty verses in Acts 7 we read Stephen's impassioned speech that led to his martyrdom. Peter's report to the church in Jerusalem following his engagement with Cornelius (Acts 11), Paul's proclamation at Antioch of Pisidia (Acts 13), and the events of the Jerusalem Council (Acts 15) are conveyed with narrative precision.[8] By contrast, Acts 18 and 19 relate only the *effects* that different kinds of speech carry in these contexts. This, I shall argue, is not peripheral to their narrative impact.

Baptismal Dialects

Even as I attempt to articulate the tone and tenor of baptismal speech in Acts 18:24–19:6, it is important to note that this is neither a typology nor a hierarchy. At most, Luke is providing us an "orderly account" (cf. Lk. 1:3) of the Holy Spirit's disorderly work in the world. The second point I wish to stress is that Luke is non-hierarchical in his descriptions of these three kinds of speech. Eloquent speech, nuanced speech, and prophetic speech each have an important role to play in the life and work of the church. It is true, as Brigitte Kahl notes, that Luke at times "opens the door" to supersessionism[9]; but

I don't believe he does so here. We ought to regard the distinctive baptismal dialects named in 18:24–19:8 as similar notes performed in a different key rather than entirely different chords.

Eloquent Speech: Mastering Discourse

Luke identifies Apollos as a Jew from Alexandria. Nowhere in his Gospel or in the Book of Acts does Luke comment upon the significance of Alexandria, nor may we determine this city's roll in his narrative imagination. Indeed, he offers only passing references to it (e.g., Acts 6:9; 27:6; and 28:11). We ought not press this point too hard, but we can imagine how this geographic detail might have resounded in the ears of Luke's listeners.

Alexandria was the epicenter of Hebrew erudition in the first century C.E. Alexandrian Jews thought and spoke in Greek, engaging their sacred texts through the Septuagint. This they would have shared with the audience Luke describes in Acts 18. Furthermore, to the degree that scholars are correct in dating the events Luke narrates in Acts, Apollos was likely a contemporary of Philo, who defended Judaism in Greek philosophical terms.[10] It is no wonder, then, that in these more heavily Hellenized regions of Ephesus (and later Corinth) that Apollos's teaching and preaching would be so warmly received by those assembled at the Synagogue in Ephesus to hear him.

Luke next declares Apollos an *eloquent* man, an ἀνὴρ λόγιος—a wordly man. This word, λόγιος, appears only here in the Greek New Testament. Whatever Luke is trying to tell us about Apollos, he wants us to know that Apollos possess an exceptional capacity for well-ordered speech. What is more, this Apollos is also *well-versed* in the Scriptures. The Greek puts it more forcefully: *being mighty (δυνατὸς) in the Scriptures*. In other words, he knew *how to do things with biblical words*. He knew how to win the synagogal language game.

Eloquent speech gives us the *proper* name for a thing, but it is precisely in this way that it structures in advance our relationship with it. Proper speech can tend to confirm what we already know; and if it does challenge knowledge, it does so within the epistemological conditions that already constitute the possibility of knowledge. The Belgian-born feminist philosopher and psychoanalyst Luce Irigaray argues that such discourse may find itself so "dragged down" or "swallowed up" by repetitions and formulas that it is unable to recognize but which nevertheless control it. Such speech proceeds by affirming itself, by maintaining the past order, and may thereby bar future discovery and insight.[11] But, astute as this observation is, it can only be made by one who has received (or honed) the capacity to listen *beyond* the dominant frame. Modifiers like "eloquent" and "powerful" only make sense comparatively—*within* a particular *episteme*.

Despite its inherent dangers, eloquent speech is crucial for contemporary Christian discourse. Some in our churches are unable to think beyond the dominant frame—not because they are incapable, but because they are inured. This is just as true of the dominant Judaisms in Luke's early first-century context as it is in our own. Pragmatically, to be eloquent and well-versed in a learned Presbyterian or astute Southern Baptist congregational context earns one a hearing. It is no small feat to convince a group of 1st century Jews that Jesus was the promised Messiah (18:28). Think of what a tremendous success it would be to help American Christians seriously grapple with white supremacy and the material inequities it fosters. Or consider the effects of challenging neoliberal assumptions concerning income disparity or the environmental impacts resulting from meat consumption and fossil fuel emissions.[12] To address such matters in a way that leads to congregational transformation would be extraordinary.

Nuanced Speech: Subverting Discourse

In addition to his ethnic background and academic pedigree, Luke tells us that Apollos had been catechized in the Way of the Lord, that he was "fervent with the (Holy) Spirit," an "accurate" (ἀκριβῶς) teacher of things concerning Jesus, and that he knew only the baptism of John. Scholarly debate abounds at this last point. Conzelmann, following Käsemann, reads v. 25 as a Lukan insertion intending to diminish without utterly obliterating Apollos's reputation *vis-à-vis* Paul.[13] Opinions vary, furthermore, regarding what Luke intends by describing Apollos as ζέων τῷ πνεύματι.[14] Is this *mere* charisma or *a God-given* charism? Fitzmyer and others suggest the latter, contending that this is an Old Testament idiom for representing God's presence.[15]

Whatever the content of Apollos's preaching, Priscilla and Aquila took issue with it. Luke fails to inform us how exactly Priscilla and Aquila explained God's way "more accurately" (ἀκριβέστερον) to Apollos.[16] Whatever instruction they convey to him seems to have been more than Apollos could bear because in the very next verse following their correction (18:27), Apollos wants to leave Ephesus for Achaia. It is noteworthy that Apollos seeks to travel to Achaia, the place where Luke has just informed us (18:12) that the Jews of Corinth "rose up with one accord" against Paul and brought him "to the place of judgment."

Chapter 18 ends with Apollos in Corinth, "vigorously defeating Jewish arguments in public debate, using the Scriptures to prove that Jesus is the Christ" (NRSV). Nowhere does Luke tell us that Apollos was (re)baptized in the name of Jesus, nor does he describe the effects of Priscilla and Aquila's teaching upon Apollos's ministry. Luke only tells us that Priscilla and Aquila received Apollos into their home and "more accurately" explained to him the way of God. Their nuanced exposition of the Way literally put Apollos "out of place" (ἐκ + τίθημι); in short, they challenged the foundational assumptions undergirding his theology.

We may only speculate as to what Paul may have discussed with Priscilla and Aquila as he stayed in their home in Corinth (18:3). Given their shared ethnic identity (as Jews), the similar social contexts in which they were reared (Pontus and Tarsus), and their shared vocation (as tentmakers), Aquila and Paul had much in common. Aquila grew up under imperial rule.[17] Luke informs us explicitly that Aquila and Priscilla were not only subjected politically but also religiously, having recently been expelled from Rome by the Emperor Claudius.

There are two points I wish to add to this discussion of Priscilla and Aquila's nuancing of Apollos's preaching. The first pertains to imperial domination, which challenges subversive speech and our reception of it. Drawing from the work of political scientist James C. Scott, Neil Elliott names the difficulties inherent in analyzing the discourse of subordinated persons. Such analyses are troubled on two fronts. On the one hand, much of what imperial subjects report must be weighed against the pervasive fear of retribution by those in power and veiled intentions to curry favor therewith. On the other hand, the official reports of imperial discourse tend to mask the true intentions of the powerful. Elliott concludes that however sophisticated our exegetical and social-scientific methods, the "public transcript" can offer only a skewed historical vision when we ignore the informal, "hidden transcripts" that could not be recorded.[18] It is not insignificant, therefore, that Priscilla and Aquila's rebuff occurs offstage. What they teach Apollos is up for debate. We may speculate about how a Jew from Alexandria—enjoying relative cultural homogeny and the right of jurisprudence—might take for granted things that Aquila and Priscilla could not.[19] To receive legal protection under Roman imperial control was a luxury of no small significance. This insight bears upon the current sociopolitical climate in the United States. Consider the disparities that persist between white people and black and brown people in the United States by the police and the justice system. Or think about how the lived experiences of transgender persons in America challenge those of cisgender persons.

The second point I wish to make in recognition of Priscilla and Aquila's nuanced speech attends to matters beyond facts and figures, beyond that which official records may deem "accurate" (ἀκριβῶς). Nuanced discourse can affirm a statement as accurate and yet name how it might also be "more accurate" (ἀκριβέστερον). Subtext matters. There is a form of knowledge accessible only to those who have endured marginalization and subjugation within a dominant epistemological/sociocultural frame. By way of illustration, Irigaray has written at length to expose androcentric and patriarchal structures that perpetuate the subordination of women. Such work cannot merely attend to published wage scales and civic opportunities. For instance, she points out that the "between-men culture" makes professional sports a universal facet of civic life. *All* are free to attend athletic matches and watch them on TV. This is true. This statement overlooks, however, the economic gap between the price paid and the product being offered. Irigaray explains that women are taxed at the same rate as men to accommodate professional sports franchises, but men are the primary beneficiaries of these venues. Thus, "economic injustice in the strict sense is reinforced by policies maintaining the illusion of egalitarianism."[20] Nuanced speech is true but on a deeper level.

Nuanced speech is liberating—to both oppressing and oppressed persons—because it gives voice to subtext. It participates in the restorative, life-giving work that Jesus came to inaugurate, since it frees the speaker to subvert the subtleties of hegemonic discourse that constitute every age and *episteme*. Nuanced speech enabled by God's Spirit shares the parlance of postcolonial and poststructural discourses inasmuch as it simultaneously participates in and yet troubles conventional speech as such.

Prophetic Speech: Transgressing Discourse

In transitioning from the Apollos narrative back to Paul (19:1), Luke tells us that Paul happens to stumble into twelve or so "disciples" who had received only John's baptism and were altogether ignorant of the Holy Spirit (19:2–3). Paul then clears up a long-standing confusion about messianic factions gathering around John (cf. Lk. 7:17–19). Paul relegates John's baptism to matters of repentance, whereas Jesus inaugurates a new kingdom with God at its head. But this interaction is more than mere substitution; salvation is not otherwise than repentance.

Those who read these verses supersessionistically, must also recognize 19:1–8 as a minority report *vis-à-vis* Luke's broader theological testimony. Baptism in the name of the Lord Jesus delivers on the prophet Joel's promise that everyone who calls on the name of the Lord shall be saved (Acts 2:21). But a strong differentiation between John's baptism (of repentance) and Jesus' baptism (unto salvation) challenges Peter's Pentecost sermon, in which Peter linked repentance with baptism in the name of Jesus Christ, whose performative effects include *both* the forgiveness of sins *and* the gift of the Holy Spirit (2:38). Would Luke have Paul place a dam where Peter built a bridge? No amount of exegetical ninjitsu can overcome this tension.[21]

The second aspect of this story that strikes me is its phenomenality. When Paul imposes his hands on these "disciples" they begin to speak in tongues and prophesy. Traditionally, scholars have associated this manifestation of the Holy Spirit with ecstatic utterances arising from "alternate" states of consciousness, which marginalizes otherness even when it aims to honor cultural difference. From their social-scientific analytic, for instance, Malina and Pilch argue that testimonies to "altered states of consciousness" must be interpreted within a given society's "consensus reality" rather than ours. While I applaud Malina and Pilch for challenging both the anachronism and ethnocentrism that would discount the empirical veracity of Luke's account from a post-Enlightenment frame, they smuggle in assumptions of their own. In naming this manifestation of the Spirit "ecstatic speech" and determining such an "alternate state of consciousness," they are able to relegate the significance of this text to communities on the fringe of ecclesial and cultural power.[22] Malina and Pilch preclude the possibility that the Spirit might enable modes of discourse able to transgress a society's epistemological strictures.

Again, to cite Irigaray, "An eidetic structure controls the functioning of our truth. No being can speak, no relation to being can be spoken, without reference to a model that determines its manifestation as approximate imitation of its ideal being." This is another way of saying what Saussure observed about linguistic structure determining—not merely expressing—thought as such. Irigaray continues, "The generic dominates the appropriation of meaning. No language is capable of speaking truth without submitting to the common-proper terms that mold it into appropriate, that is, essential, forms."[23] It is difficult, if not impossible, for us to fathom speech that transcends the very "mold" of language. What would such speech even sound like? For it to transcend epistemological conventions, and thereby transcend every prior nominalization, neither Paul, nor Luke, nor we would be able to understand it. Such speech would be altogether *other*. We would recognize such speech as a kind of language; but being beyond our linguistic capacities, we could neither name nor access its internal rationality, *viz.*, ἐλάλουν τε γλώσσαις.

The Spirit catalyzes prophecy. We must resist the temptation to read 1 Corinthians into this pericope, where tongues and prophecy occur in frequent proximity. Luke employs the verb προφητεύω only here and in 2:17–18. In both instances, prophetic speech results from the outpouring of God's Spirit. Prophetic speech is truly liberating discourse because it transcends the discursive possibilities maintained by the dominant *episteme*. Irigaray observes that "the names given to the real keep it" and hereby "the things of the universe, and we ourselves, enter into a same world thanks to a system of denominations that governs representations, and even perception."[24] I contend that any prophecy worthy of the name would require a certain glossolalia. How else might speech that announces that which is wholly other manifest itself?

CONCLUSION

We are immersed in our patterns of discourse as we are immersed in the waters of baptism. In both we are inaugurated in a kind of death. Baptismal speech is mundane speech plus something more. It carries an aural quality that differentiates itself from discourse as such. What I want preachers, teachers, and activists to think more deeply about are the ways in which our baptismal speech conforms to pre-existing modes of discourse, subverts those discursive regimes, and presages new ways of thinking and speaking beyond the dominant frame. I also wish to affirm each of these modes within particular discursive communities. Such a non-hierarchical perspective enables us to see the ways in which Luke's narrative/historical/apologetic intentions mask and reveal modes of baptismal speech "offstage" or even "behind the text."

There is a great value to theological discourse, but it is not what you *think*. Its superlative benefit for a Jesus Way of living and speaking is its capacity to rupture thought. Rupture, not penetrate. Not outside (as if any outside were not always already on the inside). A breach from within displaces and disseminates God-talk even as it opens the possibility of other ways of speaking.

Baptismal speech inaugurates the believer into a Way that is no way. It is a Way of life amid death. It pushes against that inevitability that awaits us all. Baptismal speech seizes hold of death—proleptically—and thereby relinquishes every possibility of holding on and thereby releasing us to the impossible possibility of eternal life inaugurated in Jesus' resurrection. Because of our gendered, radical, ethnic, and sex/ual particularities, our baptism into this Way cannot be universal. It must be singular.

Baptismal speech presages an alternative mode of thinking, speaking, and being in the world. Such confessional stances do not merely capitulate to dominant structures of thought, speech, and action. By entering into the waters of baptism in the name of Jesus, one dies to the systems and structures that previously governed the person's thought, speech, and action. Baptism may open us to see what has always already been at work within discursive paradigms and carries them forward within the dominant frame (eloquent speech). Baptism may enable us to subvert linguistic and logical frameworks that perpetuate the marginalization and oppression of minoritized persons (nuanced speech). Or baptism may lead us toward altogether alternative modes of discourse (prophetic speech). Only Jesus was raised to new life out of his death. And only in the name of Jesus might we die to the structures and systems that regulate our selfhood, that determine us as selves.

Out here in Asia Minor, amid great political and religious pressure, Luke affirms baptismal speech in its polyphony. Eloquent, nuanced, and prophetic speech all have a part to play within particular contexts. Likewise, in our own fraught sociopolitical contexts, I want to suggest that these three modes of baptismal speech might once again receive the church's affirmation. There is a gift to speech that participates wholly in a community's discursive norms and reflects the ideological assumptions thereof. Apollos models a kind of hermeneutical and homiletical discourse that operates within the dominant epistemological frame and speaks eloquently within that frame to strengthen Christian thought and bolster Christian engagement with the world.

Priscilla and Aquila offer an alternative mode of baptismal speech that celebrates nuance. Such resounds with the timbre of hybrid and bilingual speech that has long been employed by subjugated persons. Here the church would do well to attend to the discursive strategies of persons of color, queer-identifying persons, and subjects reared under colonial/imperial oppression. Such speech rarely manifests as a direct and unequivocal denouncement of the reigning structures; but rather, it subverts and deconstructs these systems in order to allow the subject to abide within a structure of oppression and move towards his/her/their epistemological and discursive emancipation.

Lastly, baptismal speech will not only preach that Jesus is the Messiah, using canonical texts to make our case, it will also imagine new ways of speaking, finding new tongues to inaugurate new ways of believing and behaving in the world under the power of the Spirit. Such persons will prophesy, participating in the logics that defy the reigning schemes that structure the oppression and subjugation of human and non-human others. This is kingdom speech (9:8). It turns the world upside down.

ROUNDTABLE CONVERSATION

1. Academic Disciplines and the "Receipts" They Require

Eric: Jacob, this essay provokes so much in me. Here's one place to start from my perspective as a biblical scholar. If Luke is largely responsible for the composition of the speeches in Acts, then how much can we expect that Apollos's words are Apollos's himself or Luke's? Is it necessary to evoke the work of historians? What if we focused on the literary shape of Apollos's characterization?

Jacob: Point taken. Without Luke's narration of these events we would have no access to them. And yet, I wonder how we might parse what is literary from what is historical in this pericope. For me, one of the key take-aways is that there are a number of narrative gaps in this story. We simply do not know what Apollos said that Luke deemed worthy of the title "eloquent." We have no access to the precise matters that Priscilla and Aquila disputed with Apollos. What might they have heard in his speech that didn't meet their standards? Acts does not tell us. We cannot answer these questions because Luke doesn't tell us. So, by what means do we fill those narrative gaps? In my quest for answers, history helps.

Eric: Let's consider a specific example. You make much of the experience Priscilla and Aquila had having been kicked out of Rome. Does their teaching of Apollos have something to do with their experience as refugees? You suggest it does. Your reading of how their plight might have shaped their worldview is certainly possible within the literary world Acts projects. But I don't think you need to bring in history to make this claim. That is, does Luke's literary representation of them as characters and the construction of this scene point to their experience of diaspora as key to understanding who they are and how they understand the gospel? And can we point to particular texts to help buttress this claim about the narrative?

Jacob: I acknowledge this aside that Luke makes concerning Priscilla and Aquila's expulsion from Rome; but my reading is less discriminating than yours between narrative and historical citation. Perhaps here is where our scholarly training structures our different approaches to the same end. As an interpreter, I want to "show my work," naming the ways (and sources) that shape my insights and support my conclusions. And here is where our disciplinary silos obtain despite our disciplinary overlap.

And here's the thing: as a preacher, I would totally go here in a sermon. I would not have room to unpack these three modes of baptismal speech that I describe in my essay; but I would hone in on the narrative/historical identity of Aquila and Priscilla and use this to lift up the importance of nuanced speech in and beyond the church.

As a preacher, I have aid of material conventions that do not exist in scholarly writing (unless we all agree to use hashtags and emojis). In another sermon, I might move into Apollos's Alexandrian identity in a subjunctive mood, my voice inflected with a certain tentativeness that could open imaginative possibilities for my congregants. Eric, if you heard me *preach* in this way, would it raise the same concerns for you that you have raised in response to my essay? Does the genre determine, or at least influence, whether your scholarly hackles are raised?

Eric: Great question! I think there is so much freedom in preaching. It's a freedom rooted in careful study of the biblical text. It's a freedom that has bounds. But I wonder too if preaching leans on trust a great deal, that is, the trust a community places in you by inviting you to proclaim the good news in their midst. Turning back to us then, maybe the three of us have found a way to develop that

72 Jacob D. Myers

sense of trust as we work in and across our disciplines. In the end, though, the bona fides of a biblical scholar shape so profoundly how I read a biblical text in a book like this.

Nikki: There will also be folks reading this who won't care about the arguments on which biblical scholars focus; they will care more about what you are saying broadly and the implications of your reading for the ways we think about and speak to one another. Even more, why should we place so much emphasis on the stability of scholarly writing?

Jacob: What do we think about the idea that Apollos's hometown afforded him a degree of cultural privilege?

Eric: Again, I'm a bit nervous about making that kind of statement because we don't want to read it into the text. We might consider, instead, how Apollos is connected with Alexandria *within* Acts. What evidence in Acts do we have for the cultural homogeny and jurisprudence that you see?

Nikki: I just realized something! Eric wants receipts but receipts from within the text. I wonder if it would be good to talk about this issue. We are talking about speech and the authority of voice. For Eric, proof of text matters. For Jacob, meaning matters. For me, implications matter. Embedded in this text is the problem of speculation. In full disclosure, I am frustrated by the fact that we validate certain voices and modes of thinking when they reflect Western or imperial individualist notions of epistemology. Why should credentialed scholars of the biblical text be the barometer? What are we saying, in fact, about the ways that the community can engage and learn from the text if we are constantly tripping over what Dr. So-and-so might say?

Eric: The frustration you name is important, Nikki, and one I try to teach my students to grapple with. I ask them to live in a tension when it comes to their expertise around biblical texts. Yes, they have learned the languages. Yes, they have spent years of study. But they don't hold exclusive access to what the texts might mean; they are not the sole authorities or arbiters of correct interpretation in the communities where they are called to serve. There is deep wisdom in these communities that can illuminate Scripture in ways no so-called "expert" can do. So, I really like the idea of the Holy Spirit intervening and in so doing creating a kind of ecstatic speech. The Spirit draws us *into* and *through* what we've experienced to something else, to something more. And this creates possibilities. Baptismal speech is a way to step into that mundane speech and still experience that something more.

2. Embracing Theological Imagination

Nikki: I think it's really important to talk about how we navigate norms in theology, in reading these texts and in our work more broadly. Talking about using the language of the day to say something different reminds me of the poetics minoritized people use today. This is the language we use every day to articulate something different than what others might say with the same words. Such language assumes a kind of relationality, a capacity to understand something new in the language we already know. It assumes a familiarity, a relationality which speaks to the ethics of the community.

It reminds me of a Jamaican woman that I know. She was trying on a wig and had decided against the look of the thing. In her heavy accent and with a lot of spirit, she exclaimed, "No, man, that one is too AMAZING." What she means is how "amazing" it is—dazzling to the eye, counter to normality, reflective of a certain bigness—and yet it is not what *she* wants. Such a use of language is jarring. We don't use "amazing" in that way anymore. This is not double-talk exactly but a playfulness with the multivalence of language. Maybe we should call this "harmony talk" to show how the fact that people are doing that politically in a religious context is important.

It's also important for us to talk about how the three of us have different things at stake in the reading of these texts and the doing of theology. We look for and ask for different "receipts," so to speak. In short, how do we make meaning of the text? The three of us do so very differently. How do we explain these differences? Is it the "receipts?" Is it the "implications" that differ? Or both? How does this kind of meaning-making make up a relationship of interpretation?

Here's the key point: our disciplinary imaginaries structure the kinds of things we are willing to say or hear. Eric, as a New Testament scholar, is cautious about certain historical/political reconstructions. Jacob, as a homiletician, engages scholarship with an eye to opening possibilities to imagine the world differently. I, as an ethicist, want us to be accountable to that world.

Eric: Perhaps, then, we should return to the goal of this book. The goal is not so much to make an argument *about* these texts but to make an argument about *theological speech*. The texts are suggestive toward a theological argument. They are suggesting a kind of theological imagination.

Jacob: The three of us are embodying a kind of speech that is "in tongues of mortals and angels." Mortal, insofar, as we've inherited a set of discursive practices through our academic disciplines, to be sure, but also through our cultural locatedness. We can't say *this* text is in the tongues of mortals, and *that* text is in the tongues of angels. The distinction is radically undecidable. Moreover, our engagement with these texts happens in *chronos*-time. Sometimes, God willing, we experience something else, something we may encounter only in *kairos*-time. It's in those moments of rupture as friends, colleagues, and co-readers that our imaginations are set aflame.

The conversations that produced this book could not have happened absent any one of the three of us. We speak in tongues of mortals. Yet in community—in the rupturing of our respective assumptions and the expansion of the scope of our respective theological possibilities—we said and heard something more. Our words did not magically transform from mortal to angelic, but we experienced something beyond the possibilities before any one of us. So, we are inviting readers not just to see our scholarly efforts, our conclusions about what these texts might mean for them. Instead, we are trying to live into a community wherein we wait for the in-breaking of Spirit speech, an in-breaking that occurs in the meeting of texts, peoples, places, the Spirit's subtle influence, and our stories. The work here always remains a gesture toward the tongues of angels. Our hope is that our readers might follow that gesture, discover God speaking in their midst, and raise their voices alongside others.

There is something beautiful (albeit "improper" and "indecent," à la Marcella Althaus-Reid) about speaking in tongues of mortals in relation to these sacred texts. Our willingness to expose ourselves to these moments is a way of going beyond what we can imagine or articulate.

NOTES

1. Luce Irigaray, *To Speak Is Never Neutral*, trans. Gail Schwab (New York: Routledge, 2002), 4: "There is a rupture between our own language, the language we program ourselves, and the one that comes back to us."

2. Ferdinand de Saussure, *Course in General Linguistic,* ed. Charles Bally, Albert Sechehaye and Albert Riedlinger, trans. Roy Harris (Chicago & La Salle, IL: Open Court, 1983), 66.

3. On the problems of teleology, intentionality, and time in Western discourse, see Jacques Derrida, *Specters of Marx: The State of the Debt, the Work of Mourning and the New International*, trans. Peggy Kamuf (New York: Routledge, 1994), and idem, "The Time Is Out of Joint," in *Deconstruction Is/In America: A New Sense of the Political*, ed. Anselm Havercamp (New York & London: New York University Press, 1995), 14–39.

4. Diana Butler Bass, *Grounded: Finding God in the World—A Spiritual Revolution* (New York: HarperOne, 2015), 155. See especially idem, *Christianity After Religion: The End of Church and the Birth of a New Spiritual Awakening* (New York: HarperOne, 2012).

5. "The product of an imperial age, Paul could only imagine the future in terms of the rule of a single, all-powerful lord (literally, a 'kyriarchy'). But he also bore the vital hopes and yearnings of a long-subjected people, and so the lord he expected was the benevolent and just messiah of Israel's ancient prophecies" (115).

6. Todd Penner and Caroline Vander Stichele, "Script(ur)ing Gender in Acts: The Past and Present Power of *Imperium*," in *Mapping Gender in Ancient Religious Discourses*, ed. Todd Penner and Caroline Vander Stichele (Leiden and Boston: Brill, 2007), 265.

7. Tat-siong Benny Liew, "Acts," in *Global Bible Commentary*, ed. Daniel Patte (Nashville: Abingdon Press, 2004), 422–24.

8. "The fact that as many as eight missionary speeches are recorded in Acts reflects how strategically important the use of speeches was in the missionary outreach of the Early Church." Thor Strandenaes, "The Missionary Speeches in the Acts of

the Apostles and their Missiological Implications," *Svensk missionstidskrift* 99 no. 3 (2011): 342.

9. Brigitte Kahl, "Acts of the Apostles: Pro(to)-Imperial Script and Hidden Transcript," in *In the Shadow of Empire: Reclaiming the Bible as a History of Faithful Resistance*, ed. Richard A. Horsley (Louisville: WJK, 2008), 155.

10. It was Philo who would lay the intellectual footings for the great Christian apologists: Clement, Athenagoras, Theophilus, Justin Martyr, Tertullian, and Origen (and perhaps the author of the Epistle to the Hebrews and the writer of John's Gospel). Jerome even lists Philo among the Church Fathers. Philo of Alexandria, *The Contemplative Life, Giants and Selections*, trans. David Winston (Mahwah, NJ: Paulist Press, 1981), 36.

11. Irigaray, *To Speak Is Never Neutral*, 6.

12. Neil Elliott says it best. "In the United States, we face the pervasive influence of the 'civil religion,' that peculiar hybrid of Christianity and fervent nationalism upon which U.S. policymakers draw to surround their actions with an aura of sacred legitimacy, hoping to gain the approval of the religious Right and the acquiescence of mainstream congregations." "The Apostle Paul and Empire," in *In the Shadow of Empire: Reclaiming the Bible as a History of Faithful Resistance,* ed. Richard A. Horsley (Louisville: WJK, 2008): 112–13.

13. Hans Conzelmann, *Acts of the Apostles: A Commentary*, ed. Eldon Jay App with Christopher R. Matthews, trans. James Limburg, A. Thomas Kraabel, and Donald H. Juel (Minneapolis: Fortress Press, 1987), 158.

14. Scholarly camps ramify according to how to render τῷ πνεύματι. Those arguing that Luke here intends the Holy Spirit include Ben Witherington III, *The Acts of the Apostles: A Socio-Rhetorical Commentary* (Grand Rapids: Eerdmans, 1998), 565; F. F. Bruce, *The Acts of the Apostles: The Greek Text with Introduction and Commentary* (Grand Rapids: Eerdmans, 1990), 402; I. Howard Marshall, *The Book of Acts: An Introduction and Commentary*, ed. Leon Morris, TNTC (Grand Rapids: Eerdmans, 1980), 303; and James D. G. Dunn, *The Acts of the Apostles* (Valley Forge, PA: Trinity Press International, 1996), 243.

Others contend that τῷ πνεύματι signifies a human quality (i.e., passion): Eduard Schweizer, "Die Bekehrung des Apollos, Ag. 18, 24–26," *Evangelische Theology* 15, no. 6 (1955): 251–53; Johannes Munck, *The Acts of the Apostles* (Garden City, NY: Doubleday, 1967), 183; and Joseph A. Fitzmyer, *Acts of the Apostles*, The Anchor Yale Bible, vol. 31 (New York: Doubleday, 1998), 638–39. Others remain undecided, e.g., Ernst Haenchen, *The Acts of the Apostles: A Commentary*, trans. Bernard Noble and Gerald Shinn (Philadelphia: Westminster Press, 1971), 550. While Hedlund supports the Holy Spirit interpretation, later he argues, "Luke's method of addressing the problem in his narrative is to bring Paul on the scene in Apollos' wake and immediately inquire about the Holy Spirit. By these observations and conclusions, we identify Luke's purpose for including this pericope: to address a deviant teaching, at least to some degree propagated by Apollos, which was preventing converts from receiving the Holy Spirit" (52).

15. Fitzmyer, *Acts of the Apostles*, 196. See also Robert L. Brawley, "The God of Promises and the Jews in Luke-Acts," in *Literary Studies in Acts: Essays in Honor*

of Joseph B. Tyson, ed. Richard P. Thompson and Thomas E. Phillips (Macon, GA: Mercer University Press, 1998), 281.

16. It is provocative to consider that Luke would describe his own account of the Way as ἀκριβῶς in his prologue (Lk. 1:3) and then to use the comparative form of this adverb (ἀκριβέστερον) to describe the teaching of this refugee couple only to fail to tell us how precisely their teaching is *more orderly/correct*. I am indebted to my friend and colleague Raj Nadella for this insight.

17. In the first century B.C.E. the Romans conquered Pontus—a region in northern Asia Minor situated on the coast of the Black Sea north of Cappadocia—and absorbed it into the Roman Empire.

18. Neil Elliott, *The Arrogance of Nations: Reading Romans in the Shadow of Empire*, Paul in Critical Contexts (Minneapolis: Fortress Press, 2008), 21. Cf. James C. Scott, *Weapons of the Weak: Everyday Forms of Peasant Resistance* (New Haven: Yale University Press, 1985), and idem, *Domination and the Arts of Resistance: Hidden Transcripts* (New Haven: Yale University Press, 1990).

19. On the culture and freedoms enjoyed by Jews in Alexandria see the meticulous scholarship of Louis H. Feldman, *Jew and Gentile in the Ancient World: Attitudes and Interactions from Alexander to Justinian* (Princeton: Princeton University Press, 1993), 63–69.

20. Luce Irigaray, "The Cost of Words," in *Je, Tu, Nous: Toward a Culture of Difference*, trans. Alison Martin (New York and London: Routledge, 1993), 123. See also her discussion of the illusion of women's economic independence in "Civil Rights and Responsibilities for the Two Sexes," in *Thinking the Difference: For a Peaceful Revolution*, trans. Karin Montin (New York: Routledge, 1994), 65–88.

21. Käsemann opens his essay on this pericope, writing, "Taken as an isolated passage, Acts 19:1–7 is the despair of the exegete." He proceeds to alleviate this despair by arguing that the "disciples" in reference were not followers of Jesus but of John. This, he argues, is Luke's apologetical historical reconstruction to defend "orthodox" Christianity against "heretical" countermovements. Ernst Käsemann, "The Disciples of John the Baptist in Ephesus," in *Essays on New Testament Themes*, trans. W. J. Montague (London: SCM Press, 1964), 136–48.

22. Bruce J. Malina and John J. Pilch, *Social-Science Commentary Book of Acts* (Minneapolis: Fortress Press, 2008), 185–87.

23. Irigaray, "The Language of Man," in *To Speak Is Never Neutral*, 228.

24. Luce Irigaray, *In the Beginning She Was* (London and New York: Bloomsbury Academic, 2013), 15.

Chapter Six

Wise Speech: 1 Corinthians 2:1–16

Jacob D. Myers

We cannot know the mystery of God. Anybody who claims otherwise is selling something. There are no signifiers in English or any other language that map sufficiently to the signified harbored—that is, safeguarded and persistently churning—in the name of God.[1]

Can you ever even *know* a mystery? Wouldn't that invalidate it as a mystery? Anything worthy of the designation *mystery* remains mysterious. At the heart of mystery is unknowing; our view is obstructed by a hedge of uncertainty and undecidability. Mystery abides, persisting through every rationality and our clever way with words. All the way down.

Here in 1 Corinthians 2, Paul references a *prior* visit and an *earlier* discursive encounter in which he did not proclaim God's mystery to them in "lofty words or wisdom" (ὑπεροχὴν λόγου ἢ σοφίας). Nor was his preaching marked by "persuasive words of wisdom" (πιθοῖς σοφίας λόγοις). In this anterior moment, Paul's proclamation unfolded according to a "demonstration" (ἀποδείξει) of Spirit and power. It is not that God's mystery was altogether inaccessible; rather, Paul seems to suggest that certain modes of discourse determine the possibility of receiving said mystery *as mystery*.

Post-Enlightenment humans tend to respond to mystery (of God) with "wise speech." It makes us feel smart. Whether our wise words are evangelical, progressive, Pentecostal, or queer matters little. Any mystery worthy of the name thwarts discursive attempts at wisdom. But this does little to quell our propensity to speak about that which we cannot speak; and so, like obdurate children we place our fingers in our ears, ignoring Wittgenstein's classic dictum: "What can be said at all can be said clearly and what we cannot talk about we must pass over in silence."[2] Paul's admonitions to the Corinthians reveal that we and they share much in common.

Before God's self-revelation we bear a sense of responsibility. We desire to respond to this mystery, but do we possess the *ability* to *respond* in a way or to a sufficient extent to the mystery (of God)? Apropos, Derrida writes, "The overweening presumption from which *no response will ever be free* not only has to do with the fact that the response claims to measure up to the discourse of the other, to situate it, understand it, indeed circumscribe it by responding thus *to* the other and *before* the other." Philosophy, in its loving pursuit of wisdom, and theology, with its supposed godly words, stay in business by offering better (or at least newer) ways to "measure up" to that which always already befuddles our calculus.

Derrida continues, "The respondent presumes, with as much frivolity as arrogance, that he can respond to the other and before the other because first of all he is able to answer for himself and for all he has been able to do, say, or write."[3] At this point Derrida and Paul are of one mind: to the extent that the mystery is *of* God, it remains *God's* mystery. Accordingly, any wisdom sufficient to the mystery of God remains, first and foremost, *God's* wisdom. It may only be revealed, never shown. It can only be imbibed, never distilled. It may only be inhaled, never manufactured. All we can do is bear witness to this mystery and lean into its logic beyond logic.[4]

The Apostle Paul says as much. To those at Corinth who in Christ are called to be *holy*, and perhaps even call themselves holy (cf. 1 Cor. 1:2), Paul's teaching seems quaint. You can almost see the eye rolls and sniggers from their Corinthian marble pews. Paul's thought is not up to their rigorous philosophical and rhetorical standards.[5] In their mind, he's a yokel, a bumpkin, a dilettante. But Paul refuses to capitulate to their metrics of wisdom. He will not submit to their standards of logic but points instead to the power of God. God's power, like God's wisdom, shares no part in the logics and measures of this world. Paul does not speak of empirical verifiability; he speaks of that which is ever beyond sight and sound. He does not speak of human wisdom—of political, economic, and religious power; he speaks of the power of God, which is beyond all possibility. He does not speak of knowledge; he speaks of crucifixion.[6]

GOD'S CRUCIFORM MYSTERY (VV. 1–5)

The way that Paul presents his argument in verses 1–5 preserves the mystery of God in two ways. First, Paul doubles-down on the cross of Christ as the mysterious and miraculous revelation of Godself to humankind.[7] The *mystery* of God is coterminous with the *witness* of God, and this confluence works semiologically as well as textually. A good many ancient sources render the ending of v. 1 as "the witness of God" (τὸ μαρτύριον τοῦ Θεοῦ). The UBS translation team went with "the mystery of God" (τὸ μυστήριον τοῦ θεοῦ) because it is supported by earlier, though fewer, manuscripts.[8] Conzelmann contends that it is "impossible to decide" between μαρτύριον and μυστήριον, and Thistleton urges us to abide with this scribal undecidability because "*both words*, although more especially mystery, emphasize what is conveyed in Christian proclamation is *truth revealed by God, not human opinions.*"[9] In short, our received text conditions at once a kind of knowing and a kind of unknowing; testimony itself is shrouded in mystery.

Second, what we have present to us in the text bears witness to a *prior* time and an *other* place to which we have no epistemological access. "And I having come to you" (Κἀγὼ ἐλθὼν πρὸς ὑμᾶς), begins Paul. He herby gestures toward a logic and mode of speech that *were* sufficient to the mystery of God—presumably: a "demonstration" (ἀποδείξει) of Spirit and of power.[10] But what we read *here*, in the words that make up 1 Cor. 2, are very much "plausible words of wisdom"; they are entirely oriented toward persuasion. What we have in this pericope, then, must be *other* than a "demonstration of Spirit and of power" (1 Cor. 2:4) on account of the very distinction that Paul himself makes between these discursive acts. By logical extension, since Paul's prior preaching did not employ eloquence or persuasion but rather arose out of a demonstration of Spirit and of power, what do we make of the spiritual power of Paul's words in 1 Cor. 2, since the latter *are* oriented toward persuasion?

There is a double irony here, an irony of ironies. On the one hand, our faith, the faith that might discover itself in the μυστήριον/μαρτύριον of God, ends up resting over an epistemological abyss. Because we have no access to Paul's prior speech—his earlier proclamation that took place in Corinth, which, I stress, is both *earlier* and *elsewhere*—our faith, alongside that of the Corinthians, has nowhere else to situate itself than upon Paul's words here and now, in this epistle. Thus, his logic and his rhetoric in 1 Cor. 2 supplants whatever weakness, fear, and trembling might previously have named the unnamable he now names. In other words, and following Paul's own logic, whatever presence there once was (perhaps) presents itself here in Paul's Epistle as radically absent; the *here* of Paul's discourse points to that/who is now*here* to be found except as a *trace*, an *archi-trace* eluding any possible signification.[11]

On the other hand, Paul confesses that he "decided to know nothing" (οὐ γὰρ ἔκρινά τι εἰδέναι)—nothing, that is, apart from Jesus Christ, the "having been crucified one" (τοῦτον ἐσταυρωμένον). Paul's thinking here is aporetic: it offers no (*a*) passage (*poros*). Its beginning is a dead end. For starters, as if *we* had the power to start, how can one *decide* not to know that which one knows? Knowing necessarily precedes judgment; we can refrain from speaking about something we know, but we cannot un-know what we know. We can never *judge* quickly enough to choose agnosticism. To decide is already to know.

Furthermore, Paul's word translated here as *knowing* (εἰδῶ) intermingles with the verb ὁράω, meaning *to see*.[12] Though we ought not press this overlap too hard, there is a semantic bridge between a certain seeing that becomes knowing. Bearing in mind, however, that Paul himself was not a witness to the cross, he did not *see* that of which he now speaks; hence, can he really *know* it? And maybe that is exactly the point. Maybe discourse "in tongues of angels" demands perceiving without having seen and knowing without comprehending. Perhaps to speak "in tongues of mortals," then, is to proclaim the impossibility of speaking.[13]

We ought also to consider the *instrumentality* of Paul's discourse. He says that he spoke not *in* lofty words but *in* weakness. Here he contrasts two modes of speech, and in this bifurcation, he privileges the latter over the former. By what rubric, I wonder, might Paul be able to discern which ways of speaking are sufficient to the divine mystery? Would not such modes of discourse need also to remain occluded, shrouded in mystery? Where would Paul need to stand to measure modes of discourse appropriate to God's μυστήριον/μαρτύριον? In what tongue might he speak? Is not the weakness that Paul claims—even boasts of—already a kind of strength in its very claimability and boastability?

Extrapolating from Paul's reasoning, let us imagine for a moment two language systems. The one I shall call *Loftese*; the other I shall call *Lowlese*. Now, which one allows us to articulate the mystery of God? Well, certainly not *Loftese*, for this language and its accompanying lexicon Paul dismisses out of hand. He declares such discourse insufficient—if not idolatrous—in service of proclaiming God's mystery/testimony. So, then, we must choose to speak *Lowlese*. But which lowly words are lowly enough (cf. Rom. 8:22–23, 26)? If it is the Spirit who alone can search everything, "even the depths of God" (v. 10), then how would we know if our lowly words were sufficiently low? Would we not require a certain wisdom, a certain calculus for differentiating "plausible words of wisdom" from "foolishness"? Would we not require a prior capacity for "discerning" the sufficiency of our discourse, a kind of theo-linguistic *discrimen*?

Here, I find Derrida's "hypothesis of the third language" quite helpful. By this he is not signifying a *foreign* language, one that could be juxtaposed to one's mother tongue; rather, this third language would be capable of naming a "differentiating and differentiated element, a *medium* that would not be *stricto sensu* linguistic but the middle/milieu of an experience of language that, being neither sacred nor profane, permits the passage from one to the other—and to tell one and the other, translating one into the other, appealing from one to the other."[14] To employ Derrida's insight for our understanding of 1 Corinthians, imagine that this third language were able to situate itself at once among and apart from both lofty and lowly discourse.

By invoking this third language, we would not conceive a different language that would be alien, other, to both parties. Instead, this third language gestures toward an *experience* "out of something in language" that would not yet or already be no longer wise *or* foolish (or always already both at once). Such capaciousness beyond every capacity for/with words would permit us a kind of wisdom to proclaim God's mystery without claiming to know anything or clamoring to have anything (cf. v. 16). Between Paul and his Corinthian interlocutors, then, we would need to conceive a way with words that is *simultaneously* wise and foolish (and neither wise nor foolish). It would not suffice to find their mean: a banal discourse allergic to either extreme. What we would require is an *experience* of wise foolishness or foolish wisdom, which, of course, would be oxymoronic: an unfaithful fidelity beyond fideism and perfidy. How, then, might such a "metalinguistic referee" adjudicate between those who are "spiritual" and those who are "unspiritual" (vv. 13–14)? How could such a language assert itself between and apart from foolishness and wisdom?

Some scholars argue that 1 Cor. 2:1–5 constitutes Paul's "mini-autobiography," employed here to bolster his theological prowess and defend his homiletical efficacy vis-à-vis Apollos and Peter (cf. 1:10–12).[15] Others argue that Paul is employing haggadic discursive patterns to assert his apostolic/prophetic credentials.[16] Attention to such matters overlooks a much more fundamental issue. Anything worthy of the designation "wise speech" would be incapable of asserting its wisdom or even understanding itself. If this were not so, then God's wisdom would not truly be "secret" and not really "hidden." God's wisdom would remain very much accessible to human contemplation and use. The axiomatics that would allow for such wise speech would cease to be wholly other—both in terms of its content and form, as if form and content were not always already penetrating and colluding with one another. Paradoxically, the mystery (of God) that could perhaps speak within Paul's proclamatory discourse undercuts the opposition Paul makes between lofty and lowly words. The wholly Other remains wholly other.[17]

SPEAKING GOD'S ERASURE (VV. 6–10)

Paul's treatment of wise speech raises an additional question for me. Is such discourse monotone, or might it find expression in multiple dialects? The Spirit functions for Paul (here at least) as a kind of Rosetta stone (v. 10), granting him epistemological access across the gap of unknowability (i.e., mystery). This creates a problem for him, and for we who would follow him. By what metric would he, or anyone else for that matter, possess the wisdom necessary to differentiate between that which is revealed humanly or divinely?

Classical (i.e., Western) thinking demands that the mystery of God be singular, One, undivided from itself. It is as if that "which God decreed before the ages" (v. 7) were but a single word. But if this is true, then that word which was spoken cannot be a word as such. A word is only possible as a word within a linguistic structure that necessarily precedes it. A word's *value* is only ever relative to the system that decides—by convention, in advance—its linguistic worth. As St. Augustine once observed, "Whoever, then, can understand a word, not only before it sounds, but even before the images of its sound are contemplated in thought—such a word belongs to no language."[18] How could we begin to decipher a word apart from language?

We must also consider the viability of the line Paul has drawn between two kinds of people and each party's respective capacity for wisdom. There is, here, a serious tension at work in Paul's thought. The NRSV renders these words in v. 6 substantivally, as "the mature" (τοῖς τελείοις) and "those who are doomed to perish" (τῶν καταργουμένων). Richard Hays notes the difficulty in rendering Paul's participle καταργουμένων into English. Hays recognizes an ephemeral and transitory aspect to this word, connoting impermanence. But this is not all. If we focus only on the word's lexical meaning, we fail to capture its passive verbal force, which is an important part of its sense here; the participle describes "not an innate property of the modified noun but an action performed upon it." Hays goes on to note that in the case of 1 Cor. 2:6, Paul does not only mean that the wisdom of the rulers of this age is impermanent, but also that their wisdom is "being doomed, being rendered void and done away, eschatologically, through God's act in Christ."[19]

I wish to suggest that Paul's use of καταργουμένων is best understood within what Dale Martin has identified as Paul's "apocalyptic frame," which makes hard binary distinctions untenable.[20] From Heidegger, and from later Derrida, I would argue for a close semantic congruence between καταργέω, *kreuzweise Durchstreichung*, and *sous rature*. Paul is pointing to the act of God whereby wisdom is put *under erasure*. Such wisdom is not completely abolished but remains legible even as it is being crossed-out (e.g., ~~wisdom~~).

When we speak of wisdom, we simultaneously over- and under-signify. The word and its deconstructive erasure are both necessary; both recognize and question the term's meaning and accepted use.[21] Hence, we who aim to speak of (God's) wisdom would do well to submit our wisdom to God's deconstructive erasure—particularly for those of us who wield power in inverse proportion to the amount of melanin in our skin or according to the presence of a Y chromosome. I disagree with Paul. Rather than asserting our maturity, we ought to embrace our status as καταργουμένων. This is not, I hasten to add, a strategy to deliver us to the plains of wisdom by another route but by recognizing that the very path to (God's) wisdom is *secret, hidden*, and *originary* (v. 7). Weakness, fear, and trembling, then, are not a posteriori dispositions one may assume in response to the mystery of God; they constitute the mystery of God for us, marking "a sort of relationship without relationship" between us and God's μυστήριον/μαρτύριον.[22]

PRESENTS WITHOUT PRESENCE (VV. 11–16)

In verses 11–16 Paul parses, or bifurcates, certain *faculties*. He interrogates human capacities for knowing that we know what we know. René Descartes, in his "Third Meditation," offers us a parallel reflection that illumines Paul's words here. Descartes enquires into the "true origin" of his ideas. In so doing, he draws several distinctions: between that which is internal to his selfhood and that which is external to his mind. He differentiates between "nature" (i.e., "spontaneous impulse") and "some natural light," which is beyond doubt. The idea of heat, for instance, constitutes a posteriori, "natural" knowledge, because Descartes perceives this idea as coming to him adventitiously from his experience of fire. Heat, therefore, transmits its "own likeness rather than something else."[23] Other ideas present their epistemological content along with their own verification. Descartes reasons,

> This is because there cannot be another faculty both as trustworthy as the natural light and also capable of showing me that such things are not true. But as for my natural impulses, I have often judged in the past that they were pushing me in the wrong direction when it was a question of choosing the good, and I do not see why I should place any greater confidence in them in other matters (concerning truth and falsehood).[24]

Paul and Descartes are making similar arguments. They each bear witness to a "faculty," or mechanism capable of discernment beyond mundane perception. But we have no specterscope, no *geistlich* Geiger counter to parse that which comes from within and that which comes from beyond our human minds. How do we know if our thoughts are from us or from the Spirit?

These verses raise a second issue. Paul says that those who are unspiritual do not receive the gifts of God's Spirit *for* they perceive these gifts to be foolish. A priori. The problem with this is that any gift that lives up to its name has no a priori. It must take place (if it can, in fact, take place) prior to calculation.[25] And not just for those whom Paul deems "unspiritual." If I can beat my gift-giver to the punch, so to speak, if I am able to decide *in advance* of receiving that the gift is a good gift, then have I not, in effect, destroyed the possibility of the gift as such?

Let's put this into very concrete terms. If my daughter presents me with a gift, for Father's Day perhaps, there is nothing I can do to erase the initial act of her gift-giving. Now, once I take hold of the gift I can chose to keep or discard it. That remains my right, and I must retain that right or that which I have received is no gift; I cannot be compelled to receive, by force, even by force of convention (good manners, culturally conditioned performances of kindness, etc.). If I chose to throw her gift immediately in the trash, to denounce the gift and my daughter as gift-giver, I cannot sufficiently erase the moment that preceded my calculation.

Moving back into Paul's Epistle, how might his emphasis on understanding trouble his argument? He says that the "unspiritual" do not receive the gifts of God's Spirit because they are *understood* to be foolish, and they are unable to understand them as gifts. By this logic, would this not be something other than a gift? Is it not a condition of possibility for a gift that the givee be able to recognize the gift as such? For instance, were I to stumble upon a necktie while hiking in the woods, I could not *know* that this was a gift—and much less that it was intended as a gift *for me*. To the degree that the gift is possible,[26] the gift must retain its givenness. This does not preclude the phenomenon of an anonymous gift. Let us imagine that along my hike I discover a wrapped box with my name on it. In this case, I could recognize the gift as a gift because of the contextual circumstances in play. Even though this would not conform to standard gift-giving practices in my culture, the wrapping paper, the bow, the label indicating me as the addressee supplement the gift itself (the necktie) and thereby constitute my recognition of the gift.

If God choses the designation Giver, there is no place we can hide, there is no fortification strong enough to obviate our designation as givees: as recipients of a gift. Moreover, Paul says that those who are spiritual "discern all things." How does such (spiritual) discernment permit a person to arrive in advance of God's gift? If Paul meant what he said in verse 7, that God's wisdom was decreed "before the ages," then this would also have to be anterior to any possibility of discernment on our part. One may only discern according to metrics and axioms that *precede* the act of discerning. Much as an act of language is impossible before the introduction of linguistic structure, so too, an *act* of discernment presupposes a *framework* for discernment as such.[27]

In verse 13, Paul suggests that because he has received the Spirit of God, he has found a way around the aporias created by mere human wisdom. Thus, he is capable of producing wise speech suitable for "interpreting spiritual things to those who are spiritual using a spiritual language."[28] Again, Derrida is helpful for our purposes because he has addressed the possibility of writing and speaking in a language that is at once necessarily (and) never quite one's own. What Paul is doing here in drawing hard distinctions between a "spiritual language" that is wise and an "unspiritual" language that is foolish. There is a profound (Western) desire to preserve an imagined purity on the inside (of language) from a contaminant on the outside. Derrida reads this gesture in the works of some of the most influential voices in Western thought (e.g., Plato, Kant, Husserl, Heidegger, Rousseau, Saussure).[29]

On one occasion, Derrida takes up a 1926 letter written in German from Gershom Scholem to Franz Rosenzweig. Of utmost concern for Scholem is the "secularization" of the (sacred) Hebrew language that the Zionists began to employ in secular discourse between the wars. Derrida writes in response to an imagined "sacred language" that might be differentiated from "secular language." He writes, "To comport oneself, to bring oneself to it [sacred language], to carry oneself toward it—this is still to comport oneself *in* it, still to speak it, even if to deny it. One cannot avoid speaking the sacred language, one can at most *avoid* speaking it, which is to say still speaking it in denial, avoidance, distraction, like sleepwalkers above the abyss."[30]

Mutatis mutandis, Paul's differentiation between "words taught by human wisdom" and "words taught by the Spirit" comes undone by its very operation. To situate wisdom within a *spiritual tongue,* whether as an innate capacity or taught by the Spirit, is to always already participate in said wisdom. To proclaim that the mystery of God can neither be spoken nor proclaimed cannot excise us from the mystery itself because the same discursive frame originarily binds us in and by it. In other words, it cannot be the case that there are some who are "mature" (τελείοις) and others who are "doomed to perish" (καταργουμένων), or that there are some who are "spiritual" (πνευματικῶς) and others who are "unspiritual" (ψυχικὸς); rather, the mystery of God produces conditions of possibility for this supposed differentiation. It is in the act of proclaiming the mystery of God as such, as that which exists in and for itself, that Paul can even discern between lofty words and lowly words. Paul need not fear that his interlocutors' (or our) faith rests on *either* human wisdom *or* on the power of God. Our speech rests on the undecidability between human wisdom and the power of God. There is no wise speech. There is only the mystery (of God).

CONCLUSION: COMING (TO) UNDONE

The phenomenality of God is the mystery of God. It remains always and forever impossible—not because we do not (yet) fully understand it, but because

God remains radically other. Only a language capable of (an/re)nouncing God's mystery would suffice. But how to announce *while* renouncing? Only *a way* with words that did *away* with words would be up for the task.

I wonder if the problem with most interpretations of these verses is that too many scholars read them synchronically rather than diachronically. To diminish the temporal dynamism at work within this text is to rob it of its life-force. To speak the impossibility of God's mystery is still to speak God's mystery. From the originary wisdom of God to the eschatological hope we find in God, we are free to enjoy the gifts of the Spirit, our discursive intermediary, our translator, who alone is able to negotiate the tensions between this age and the age to come, between foolishness and wisdom, between secrecy and revelation. Either there exists a wisdom to which we have access and that precedes God's wisdom, or this is nothing more than Pauline hocus pocus. God's wisdom collapses into mere rhetoric. Or, as theologian Philipp Stoellger puts it: "all that remains is to trust in the power of the word (*Wortmacht*), instead of claiming a divine word of power (*Machtwort*)."[31]

Any claim to "wise speech" renders itself mute and meaningless. There is, as Derrida observes, "division and iterability of the source." In other words, it is on account of the irreducible otherness originary to the cross of Christ that Paul is even able to differentiate between the wisdom of God and the wisdom of this age. "This supplement introduces the incalculable at the heart of the calculable."[32] Wise speech falters when it boasts in itself (cf. 1:29, 31), but these impossibilities need not silence us. There is hope for the possibility of wise speech in its impossibility. In weakness, fear and trembling, with stutters and stammers and false starts symptomatic of a kind of aphasia, the wisdom (of God) may be uttered—perhaps.

The tongues of mortals at once give and take language from us. Because we do not chose our native language, our mother tongue, we are incapable of ever stepping outside its system and sounds. The gift of language gives us the capacity to think and to speak even as it robs us; it incapacitates us from thinking or speaking otherwise.[33] We are *thrown* into "absolute translation, a translation without a pole of reference, without an originary language, and without a source language."[34] But the realization of this truth, this always already aspect of linguistic structure, need not produce spiritual quiescence.

By gesturing toward another time and a place (v. 1) and pointing an eschatological finger to a destination beyond seeing, hearing, and perceiving (v. 9), Paul offers us a path *toward* wise speech that appears nowhere *in* his epistle. It is not enough to invert the reigning sociocultural epistemology: to supplant strength for weakness, folly for wisdom, etc. Such would leave the binary system intact; saying "no" to the terms of the opposition is still to say "yes" to the opposition that produced the possibility of rejection. With Derrida and according to an oblique reading of Paul, I wish to forward a mode of discourse for proclamation in and beyond the church that is not quite "mature" (τελείοις), one that is not so sure about where it will end (τέλος). This may sound a little weak (ἀσθένεια) and kind of foolish (μωρός)—mad, even. I may sound like one who is "coming undone" (καταργουμένων). But this is what a "demonstration of the Spirit and power" (ἀποδείξει Πνεύματος καὶ δυνάμεως) looks and sounds like. To come to speech, in "fear and much trembling" (φόβῳ καὶ ἐν τρόμῳ πολλῷ), before the mystery (of God) that is originarily held "in secrecy and hiddenness" (ἐν μυστηρίῳ, τὴν ἀποκεκρυμμένην), requires a "thinking of language, an experience of language that enables a deconstruction of the philosophical oppositions that govern" it.[35]

Discourse that participates in God's μυστήριον/μαρτύριον shares in God's wisdom according to a "silent performative," an "unpronounceable 'yes'" that is neither present nor object nor subject," and is therefore neither ontological nor transcendental.[36] There "is" no wisdom of God that we may know or about which we may speak. Our proclamation, therefore, can only ever come undone in its very coming.

ROUNDTABLE CONVERSATION

1. Textual Engagement, or How Do We Ever Even Read a Text?

Eric: I was particularly intrigued by the text critical work this chapter lifts up. So often, text critical work is seen as this dusty, technical pursuit. Sometimes, scholars and students have seen textual criticism as prolegomenon to exegesis but not exegesis itself. It is science, not a theological pursuit. But it's always been way more than that and actually far more interesting than that. Indeed, a number of text critical scholars have seen this all along, I think; but perceptions about text criticism have remained far less complex than its actual practice. Jacob, you help us see the complexities of texts themselves. That the textual witness itself participates in the mystery is key. For some, text criticism is the establishment of an original text or at least an initial text. But what if textual criticism is, in a way, always destabilizing the text itself? For many of us, interpretation has felt unstable or at least tenuous. I could be reading a text incorrectly; someone might have a better reading than I do. But what if we remember that the text itself is a negotiated, eclectic mix of many manuscripts? What if we are dealing with texts every time we read "a" text? That is, reading a text is even more complex than we have first acknowledged. And in that complexity, we have to do a lot of theology if we hope to engage in any kind of God-talk.

Nikki: I have always approached the text in the way that you are describing, Eric; it feels very familiar to me. If I did not approach it with this kind of criticism, I was always positioned in opposition to the text. We, the text and I, were problems for one another. So, the kind of textual criticism that that you illustrated, Jacob, and that you describe, Eric, is what I used as a way to figure out what was really being said to *and* for me. And, I had to reconcile that those were not always the same thing. Such a process helped me choose what kind of relationship I could have with Paul's letters or any other text. I would distinguish between what the text ways saying and what it implied. I would make note of how people in various contexts typically made meaning of the text and think about what made them take it seriously.

And here's the other thing. We should pay attention to the kinds of realities that make it necessary for a person or community to discover, hone, and employ this approach as they encounter sacred texts. How does that impact their relationship to the material? What funds the process? What hinders it? If we pay attention to those questions, we might recognize the importance and outcomes of different folks' textual strategies. We might, more simply, be honest about our commitments.

Jacob: When I was first introduced to textual criticism, a hard line was established between exegesis and eisegesis. The problem with this distinction is that it can be wielded as a bludgeon to bash divergent interpretations to bits. Nikki, I appreciate you sharing your affinity with this mode of textual engagement because the approach I take to the text in this essay would've been utterly inconceivable to my undergrad self. I have been accused of reading the text too much against the grain (which goes hand-in-hand with the charge of eisegesis). But something spiritual happens when we slow way down and attend to what is actually happening in the text. It exposes our assumptions. It challenges our prejudices. I find that my (erotic) approach to biblical interpretation (see my *Making Love with Scripture: Why the Bible Doesn't Mean How You Think It Means*), helps me to catch a glimpse of something happening in the text that is always skittering beyond my angle of vision. It's like a whisper that you can only barely perceive, drawing you in even closer.

Eric: In the end, I find the distinction between exegesis and eisegesis unavailing, particularly if we assume that the difference between the two is reading *in* versus reading *into*. The distinction I first learned was that exegesis was reading authorial intent, basically. The text means what it means. Eisegesis reads *into* the text our own hopes, desires, questions, whatever. But what if all reading is eisegetical because all reading inevitably brings with it all our "stuff," so to speak: race, ethnicity, gender, sexuality, experiences. None of that "stuff" is separable. And thus all exegesis is also eisegesis under that strict distinction. But what if all that "stuff" is not just an accretion of obstacles on our way to exegesis but assets for faithful reading?

Jacob: Well said, Eric! Here we might be able to reflect together on how we move from texts to God-talk. The text challenges the epistemological ground upon which we stand. No one cultural or epistemological standpoint can claim ownership of a "right" way of reading. It is in the cracks and the gaps that the text creates among and within us that we receive the capacity for God-talk.

Nikki: Do you think there are biblical scholars who will say, "Fine, think what you want but the text says what it says?" They might also say, "Relate to it how you want, but this is what the text says." What investment is behind that kind of question or statement?

Jacob: This chapter troubles a "this is what the text means" standpoint. There are textual variants. There is an apophatic naming of a threshold that we can see as threshold but cannot cross. Might this book inspire some cross-disciplinary teaching and learning that could help students, pastors, scholars, and activists explore new discursive possibilities? I think that this approach can be especially generative among teachers and learners with very different cultural perspectives. When we double-down on a rigid understanding of biblical meaning, we miss the work of the Spirit among us. This is impossible to name; it can only be experienced, and only then in a community that affirms the beauty of difference. Even when we (you, Eric, and I) have shared moments when we feel like we are approaching the tongues of angels, in seeking to capture those experiences they escape our grasp: they become words of mortals once again.

2. Now That We've Read, What Can We Do?

Eric: And yet, the text critical stuff is only scratching the surface. It's pulling a thread. The textual variant is a concrete example of the tenuousness of the text and so also then the tenuousness (and attendant richness!) of our interpretations.

Jacob: I'm trying to model a way of being/becoming with biblical texts that can be life-giving for teachers, preachers, and activists. I hope to shift the conversation away from a "this is what the text says and this is how we should apply it" frame. In my essay, I seek to offer a way of entering into the text obliquely that troubles the assembly line or conveyor belt approach to hermeneutics and homiletics. We can give our communities and congregations a way of not assimilating Paul's proclamation. If I were to preach this pericope, that might be a whole sermon, just that one insight.

Also, what I've tried to do is to choose an interlocutor. Here, I chose Derrida to show how a certain orientation to scripture can inform—and perhaps transform—the way we engage it. This is the challenge. It is a fundamental critique of the whole enterprise of theological discourse and the techniques we learn in religion departments and seminaries about how we ought to engage texts. If I were teaching the biblical text, I would have students slow down with it. Such an approach is not just for biblical scholars. It reveals the textual ambiguity that has been hidden from our view by well-intentioned biblical translators, teachers, and preachers. This teaches students how to receive canon—political and institutional—with a certain wariness, to see what is being masked.

Eric: That is, the text starts to fall apart as we get closer to it. How is that encounter with the text helping us to speak something different?

Jacob: What I'm showing with Paul is a way of taking seriously what he's saying. I then ask, what are you allowing to be hidden in order to let the text speak? This disturbs the assumption that the preacher goes to the text to mine its meaning for a sermon. An illustration of what I'm getting at here is in the sixth Harry Potter book and movie. In *The Half-Blood Prince,* Harry attempts to pull a locket from a basin full of water. He cannot take hold of the locket or get rid of the water. Dumbledore then realizes that the only way for the water to go away (and thereby retrieve the locket) is for one of them to drink it. I like this metaphor because it illustrates both our desire to receive from the text and the risks inherent with our engagement. Moreover, we must allow the text to enter us in some sense, without any guarantees, backups, or safety nets. I think about how certain readings can be noxious to particular ways of being or relating to others; at the same time, other readings can be life-giving and liberating.

Eric: Theological educators have tended to teach preaching and biblical studies as solitary acts of digging. That is, what we learn in the biblical studies classroom is how to use certain tools to dig into the text. I have a shovel, a spade that helps me dig into the text and discover the truth of this text under all the exegetical dirt. And the underlying assumption is that I can do that kind of digging/reading on my own. All I need is a shovel and the text to discern its truth. The kinds of readings we are performing in this book are different. It imagines a drinking of the text alongside others. It imagines that what we learn in a biblical studies classroom is not the use of certain tools but the honing of an imaginative sensibility that reads texts *and* the readings of those texts by others with grace and a critical eye, curiosity and attention to the stories our neighbors tell, trust and suspicion.

Nikki: I agree (and appreciate that metaphor), Eric. Can we imagine this book being used in academic spaces beyond theological studies? What about, say, women's studies or sexuality studies? If I choose to use this book in an "unrelated" field, I am illustrating an unapologetic commitment to fully engaged, integrity-filled, cross-disciplinary learning and teaching. I would not be leaving my "home field" to do this kind of work; rather; I'd be enhancing my groundedness while reaching out and across constructed (and often unhelpful lines) to learn and teach something new. I think that this is an ethical approach to scholarship and a way of being *better informed* conversation partners with one another.

NOTES

1. Jacques Derrida, the eminent Franco-Maghrebian philosopher and literary theorist, informs my thinking here: "Every negative sentence would already be haunted by God or by the name of God, the distinction between God and God's name opening up

the very space of this enigma." Jacques Derrida, "How to Avoid Speaking: Denials," in *Derrida and Negative Theology*, ed. Harold Coward and Toby Foshay (Albany: State University of New York Press, 1992), 76.

2. Ludwig Wittgenstein, *Tractatus Logico-Philosophicus*, trans. B. F. McGuinness and D. F. Pears (London: Routledge, 1961), 3.

3. Jacques Derrida, "Passions: "An Oblique Offering," in *On the Name*, ed. Thomas Dutoit, trans. David Wood (Stanford: Stanford University Press, 1995), 20.

4. But here to lean into a logic is to attend to what Derrida will associate with the middle voice, with a certain *désisitance* that troubles both the constitution of a speaking subject who *consists* and *desists* under the guise of negative theology. See Jacques Derrida, "Désistance," in *Psyche: Inventions of the Other, Volume II*, ed. Peggy Kamuf and Elizabeth Rottenberg, trans. Christopher Fynsk (Stanford: Stanford University Press, 2008), 196–230.

5. Scholarly debate proliferates concerning Paul's use and theology of rhetoric vis-à-vis that of the Corinthians. See Benjamin Fiore, "The Hortatory Function of Paul's Boasting," *Proceedings* 5 (1985): 39–46; Peter Marshall, *Enmity in Corinth: Social Conventions in Paul's Relations with the Corinthians* (WUNT II/23; Tübingen: J.C.B. Mohr, 1987); Timothy H. Lim, "Not in Persuasive Words of Wisdom, but in the Demonstration of the Spirit and Power," *Novum Testamentum* 29 (1987): 137–49; Stephen M. Pogoloff, *Logos and Sophia: The Rhetorical Situation of 1 Corinthians* (SBLDS 134; Atlanta: Scholars Press, 1992); Duane Litfin, *St. Paul's Theology of Proclamation* (SNTSMS 79; Cambridge: Cambridge University Press, 1995); Michael A. Bullmore, *St. Paul's Theology of Rhetorical Style: An Examination of 1 Corinthians 2:1–5 in the Light of First Century Graeco-Roman Rhetorical Culture* (San Francisco: International Scholars Publications, 1995); Matthew R. Malcolm, *Paul and the Rhetoric of Reversal in 1 Corinthians: The Impact of Paul's Gospel on His Macro-Rhetoric* (SNTSMS 155; Cambridge: Cambridge University Press, 2013).

6. John Barclay observes, "The wisdom of the cross is not just an alternative wisdom but an anti-wisdom, rebutting or subverting what would normally be taken for granted. . . . To align oneself with the message of Christ crucified is not just to sidestep the framework of the world, but to disturb its claims and to confront its hegemony: 'if anyone thinks he is wise in this age, *let him become a fool*, in order that he may be wise' (3:18)." John M. G. Barclay, "Crucifixion as Wisdom: Exploring the Ideology of a Disreputable Social Movement," in *The Wisdom and Foolishness of God: First Corinthians 1–2 in Theological Exploration*, ed. Christophe Chalamet and Hans-Christoph Askani (Minneapolis: Fortress Press, 2015), 5. I find this epistemological argument more compelling, and more consistent with Paul's broader intentions in 1 Cor. (esp. in chs. 12–14), than those suggesting that Paul is performing under the guise of a "befuddled orator." Cf. L. L. Welborn, *Paul, the Fool of Christ: A Study of 1 Corinthians 1–4 in the Comic-Philosophic Tradition* (JSNTSS 293; London and New York: T & T Clark International, 2005), 92.

7. Pickett is right to argue that the cross constitutes "the crux" of Paul's argument to the Corinthians. Raymond Pickett, *The Cross in Corinth: The Social Significance of the Death of Jesus* (JSNTSS 143; Sheffield, UK: Sheffield Academic Press, 1977), 77. So, too, Malcolm, 163: "The cross provides the focal point for human derision

of God (perhaps in the very act of straining to know him [*sic*]) at the same time as providing the vehicle for humans to receive God's saving power. In this sense it [the cross] acts negatively to demolish human attempts at knowledge of God, but positively to offer graciously that very knowledge, *from God.*"

8. Especially P46 and א. See Bruce M. Metzger, *A Textual Commentary on the Greek New Testament*, 2nd ed. (New York: American Bible Society, 1994), 480.

9. Hans Conzelmann, *1 Corinthians: A Commentary*, Hermeneia, trans. James W. Leitch (Philadelphia: Fortress Press, 1975), 53, n. 6; Anthony C. Thistleton, *The First Epistle to the Corinthians*, NIGTC (Grand Rapids, MI: Eerdmans; Carlisle, Cumbria: Paternoster Press, 2000), 207–8.

10. The word ἀποδείξει is *hapax legomenon* in the New Testament. Lim, 147, citing texts by Diogenes Laertius, Plato, and Cicero, notes that this was a technical rhetorical term connoting a "demonstration or cogent proof of argument from commonly agreed premises." Lim contends that by conjoining this technical term with Πνεύματος and δυνάμεως, Paul is flipping this term on its head: "This demonstration does not consist of arguments from generally accepted truths, but upon the divine conviction of the Spirit and power (cf. 1 Cor. 4:20)."

11. See Jacques Derrida, *Positions*, trans. Alan Bass (Chicago: The University of Chicago Press, 1981), 19.

12. See Friedrich Blass, Albert Debrunner, and Robert W. Funk, *A Greek Grammar of the New Testament and Other Early Christian Literature* (Chicago: The University of Chicago Press, 1961), §81, 3.

13. Peter Lampe gets it right when he declares that "precisely *because* God is absolute, the human speech about God cannot be. According to the text, any human theology is moved into constant crisis by its own subject for discussion—by God. This subject in its power (*dynamis*, 1:18, 24) constantly withdraws itself from human theology, putting up resistance against domestication. Trembling (2:3) would be the correct attitude of the theologian." Peter Lampe, "Theological Wisdom and the 'Word about the Cross': The Rhetorical Scheme in 1 Corinthians 1–4," *Interpretation* 44, no. 2 (April 1990): 122.

14. Jacques Derrida, "The Eyes of Language: The Abyss and the Volcano," in *Acts of Religion*, ed. and trans. Gil Anidjar (New York and London: Routledge, 2002), 200.

15. Adam G. White, "Not in Lofty Speech or Media: A Reflection on Pentecostal Preaching in Light of 1 Cor 2:1–5," *Journal of Pentecostal Theology* 24, no. 1 (2015): 122.

16. Wilhelm H. Wuellner, "Haggadic Homily Genre in 1 Corinthians 1–3," *Journal of Biblical Literature* 89, no. 2 (June 1970): 199–204.

17. See Jacques Derrida, *The Gift of Death; and Literature in Secret*, 2nd ed., trans. David Wills (Chicago and London: The University of Chicago Press, 2008), 82–84: "Every other (one) is every (bit) other" [*Tout autre est tout autre*].

18. Augustine, *On the Trinity: Books 8–15*, ed. Gareth B. Matthews, trans. Stephen McKenna (Cambridge: Cambridge University Press, 2002), XV.19, p. 186. By this, he clarifies, "to none of the so-called national languages, of which ours is Latin."

19. Richard B. Hays, *Echoes of Scripture in the Letters of Paul* (New Haven and London: Yale University Press, 1989), 134.

20. Dale B. Martin, *The Corinthian Body* (New Haven and London: Yale University Press, 1995), 62. Martin explains that while Paul invokes a dualism (this world/ other world), this dualism does not fit neatly into an ontological division between natural and supernatural forces: "No concept of 'mere' politics understood independently of higher cosmic conflicts is possible in Paul's thinking. For Paul, 'this world' is not the closed system of nature but the dark, confused world of rebellion against God."

21. Derrida articulates this deconstructive erasure through a radical kind of *play*. See Jacques Derrida, *Of Grammatology*, trans. Gayatri Chakravorty Spivak, corrected ed. (Baltimore: The Johns Hopkins University Press, 1976), 50.

22. On the "relationship without relationship" in relation to a priori structures that always already confine us, see Jacques Derrida, *Monolinguism of the Other; or, The Prosthesis of Origin*, trans. Patrick Mensah (Stanford: Stanford University Press, 1998), 71.

23. René Descartes, "Third Meditation," in *Meditations on First Philosophy: With Selections from the Objections and Replies*, ed. and trans. John Cottingham (Cambridge: Cambridge University Press, 1996), 26.

24. Ibid., 27. Later, in his reply concerning objective reality, Descartes adds, "Now this mode of being is of course much less perfect than that possessed by things which exist outside the intellect; but, as I did explain, it is not therefore simply nothing" (86).

25. Recently, John Barclay has argued that the gift's impossibility is not "a natural or necessary construal of the gift" but a late construction "reflecting a modern ideological polarization between freedom and obligation, interest and disinterest." Barclay concludes, "In any case, we should be conscious that, despite the enormous influence of Bourdieu and Derrida, it would be arbitrary to make the absence of reciprocity and 'self-interest' the very essence of the gift." John M. G. Barclay, *Paul and the Gift* (Grand Rapids: Eerdmans, 2017), 63. While he is right to assert that this "peculiarly modern presumptions does *not* correspond to the assumptions of antiquity and should not be allowed to determine what Paul or his fellow Jews might have understood by the grace or gifts of God" (185), Barclay, peculiarly, fails to consider Paul's treatment of spiritual gifts in 1 Corinthians, much less the situation whereby one judges (ἀνακρίνει) and refuses the gifts of God's Spirit (2:14–15).

26. See Jacques Derrida, *Given Time: I. Counterfeit Money*, trans. Peggy Kamuf (Chicago and London: The University of Chicago Press, 1992). He concludes, "For this is the impossible that seems to give itself to be thought here: These conditions of possibility of the gift (that some 'one' gives some 'thing' to some 'one other') designate simultaneously the conditions of the impossibility of the gift . . . these conditions of possibility define or produce the annulment, the annihilation, the destruction of the gift" (12).

27. Ferdinand de Saussure puts it this way: "In itself, thought is like a swirling cloud, where no shape is intrinsically determinate. No ideas are established in advance, and nothing is distinct, before the introduction of linguistic structure." *Course in General Linguistics*, ed. Charles Bally, Albert Sechehaye, and Albert Riedlinger, trans. Roy Harris (Chicago: Open Court, 1983), 66.

28. There is an interesting, and I believe theologically rich, textual variant in v. 13. Is it "interpreting spiritual things to those who are spiritual," "interpreting spiritual things

in spiritual language," or "comparing spiritual things with spiritual"? See Thistleton, 264–67 for a list of scholarly interpretations of this semantically undecidable verse.

29. See Derrida, *Of Grammatology*; idem, *Speech and Phenomenon: And Other Essays on Husserl's Theory of Signs*, trans. Dale B. Alison (Evanston, IL: Northwestern University Press, 1973); and idem, *Margins of Philosophy*, trans. Alan Bass (Chicago and London: The University of Chicago Press, 1982).

30. Derrida, "The Eyes of Language," 202.

31. Philipp Stoellger, "The Word of the Cross in the Conflict of Interpretive Power: On the Genealogy of Theology Deriving from the Spirit of Pauline Rhetoric," in *The Wisdom and Foolishness of God*, 207. Later in his essay, Stoellger makes this case even stronger: "Between divine power at the origin and the claim to power in the word of power (*Machtwort*) of the apostle, there is a third player, namely the powerful word (*Wortmacht*), that is, the word's own intrinsic dynamic—whose power of conveying and convincing is bet upon: on the word's interpretive power. The critical question for any theology is, therefore: Does one stay with the powerful word's weakness, or does one claim more in order to secure it further, be it with words of power or on the basis of an original power (with a final explanation free from interpretation)?" (217).

32. Derrida, "How to Avoid Speaking," 100.

33. Derrida, *Monolinguism of the Other*, 39: "All culture is originarily colonial. . . . Mastery begins, as we know, through the power of naming, of imposing and legitimating appellations."

34. Ibid., 61.

35. Derrida, "The Eyes of Language," 224.

36. Jacques Derrida, "A Number of Yes," in *Psyche: Inventions of the Other, Volume II*, 238–39.

Chapter Seven

Loving Speech: 1 Corinthians 13:1–13

Thelathia "Nikki" Young

Each year during Mother's Day weekend, I post a Facebook message that allows me to participate in the cultural practice of appreciating mothers and mothering. Since my mother passed away when I was in college, my posts often reflect some memory that I have of her or articulate a lesson that she taught me. This year, I posted about my experience of her love:

> This semester has been the most. Usually when I say that, the connotation leans toward the negative, but ON TODAY (because I'm southern and occasionally churchy) I mean it in the most delicious way. . . . I had a major surgery. I gave public talks and published a couple articles. I found dope records and read a few amazing books. I saw friends and chosen family, and I connected with my bio-kin. I experienced grace and gave some back. I helped students grow. I laughed.
>
> In response to such a semester, I can only give thanks (like my mommy taught me to do). So . . . Benae, you are the truth. My recovery is owed in large part to your perfect loving care and to your brilliance when teaching my class (which freed me from worry). Thank you. Also, Lewisburg peeps, thank you for caring for our animals and bringing us food and sending flowers and notes and dropping by and just showing us so much love. And folks who don't live here, thank you for the cards and calls and gifts and offers to visit. To my colleagues whose emails I am just now reading and responding to, thank you for your continued grace and patience.
>
> And to my mom: I see you. Thank you for loving me across time and space and realms. Thank you for these gifts of manifested love. And thank you for reminding me always to show such love while dripping swaggoo. #mommyinginfinitely #lovewithoutlimit[1]

With this post, I wanted to offer appreciation for love that I could *feel*. I experienced a variety of gifts—generosity, comfort, grace, compassion, and more—but they held meaning for me only inasmuch as they were tangible manifestations of love. I wanted to honor the gift that I felt my mother present from a different realm: divinely filling and eternal love that surpasses rational knowledge of any boundary between us.[2]

Paul's loving speech in 1 Corinthians 13 highlights such love. It flows directly from his explanation about the body of Christ in the previous chapter, in which he explains to the church in Corinth that they are all necessary parts of one body. While that chapter describes how their community is or ought to be comprised, chapter 13 delineates how they ought to *relate* to and with one another. For Paul, the only viable option is love.

Paul establishes love (*agape*) as both the goal and the path, and while he does not use the term, I assert that he establishes the importance of *agape* so by making space for *eros*. *Eros* is the means by which people see, feel, and understand *agape*. Paul does not want an intangible love to govern the people; instead, he advocates for a love that allows for the fullness of their humanity. Only love that they can feel and that calls them into mutual revelation will reflect the divine. In the following pages, I walk through the ways that Paul establishes *agape*'s importance and illustrates how it might be the "more excellent way." I consider how love is transgressive, as it breaks down multiple boundaries and disestablishes hierarchies. I also talk about how Paul relates love to knowledge, which, in the context of this Greek metropolis, is valued as the highest good. Paul draws a bridge between knowledge and love, and I suggest that the bridge is love as self-revelation (a different kind of gnosis). Such love allows folks to co-create the subjects that then comprise the body of Christ—a divine process indeed. I further claim that while Paul encourages divine love, mutual self-revelation is made known through our senses and experiences; therefore, I conclude the chapter by arguing that erotic love is a part of the divine love scheme.

TRANSGRESSIVE LOVE

As a black queer ethicist, one of the things that I look for when reading any text (and especially biblical text) is whether or not the writer (or speaker in the text) is using language to reinforce injustice and hegemonic forces or subvert and resist them. There are a few possible ways to read 1 Corinthians.[3] One way is to recognize that there was tension among members who were thought to possess differing levels of spiritual wisdom, as evidenced by speaking in tongues or prophesying. With demonstrably high value in Corinth, wisdom represented (for centuries) the "highest good" toward which humans ought to strive. This reading situates Paul's speech in the letter as a strong suggestion for a shift in values and virtues among the members of the church. Another reading recalls that Corinth was a multi-religious environment, and therefore Paul's letter is about maintaining boundaries around the body (the temple) within a pluralist context. A third way to read it is by remembering that the citizenry of Corinth was composed of former slaves and immigrants, rendering the socio-historical context quite diverse but also steeped in Roman colonialism and imperialism. In this context, then, Paul's letter would have been a description of how and why the church in Corinth stood in alterity (and perhaps even opposition) to established social boundaries.

My encounter with Paul in 1 Cor. 13 combines each of those reading possibilities, especially the first and third that I list above. I see Paul doing theologically important and socio-politically difficult work. I see him calling for a nuanced view of love that works against established norms and social scripts. Paul introduces this section of the letter with the last sentence of the previous chapter: "But strive for the greater gifts. And I will show you a still more excellent way" (1 Cor. 12:31). The previous chapter, which is about spiritual gifts, explains how people with different gifts may contribute to and be a part of the body of Christ. The spirit is given for the purpose of (perhaps, to serve) the common good (12:7).[4] The notion of the common good is illustrated in multiple ways, not the least of which is by means of caring for the vulnerable (those who "seem to be weaker are indispensable" 12:22–24). Paul continues this subversive theme in 12:24 with the phrase "greater honor to inferior members" where each is to care for one another the same (12:25).

I do find it odd that, after all this, Paul seems to leave room for a hierarchical understanding of body parts (i.e., referring to some as "weaker"). It is no wonder, then, that in the last verse, which affirms that there are differentials in the greatness of gifts, Paul alludes to a way to nullify the hierarchy altogether. Although his method for highlighting differences in the body is embedded in a set of presumed hierarchies that are based on differentials in gifts' value, I still appreciate what he is trying to do. In chapter 13, Paul both responds to dissension among people in the church and tries to teach them how to be in community with one another. Even more, Paul creates a moral system that aims to benefit the whole community through the collective and integrative work, responsibility, and vulnerability of its members. He establishes a social ethic that is based on the common good as telos and interdependence as ethos.

For Paul, love is the "more excellent way" that neutralizes the impact of a social hierarchy by eliminating envy, boastfulness, arrogance, irritation, and resentment (13:4–5). The nullification of the hierarchy seems more important an issue than the erasure of difference, and the dissolution of the boundaries comes through the elimination of the power dynamics that such boundaries foster. Paul conveys this point by clarifying the difference between gifts that are incomplete/partial/imperfect and those that are complete/whole/and perfect. For him, this set of distinctions gives meaning to the ethos of the *ekklēsia*, an ethos that is as much about the future as it is about the present. And, to be clear, Paul speaks of the future in two ways: the *telos* (the end) and the *eschaton* (the goal). With this distinction, Paul illustrates the difference between completion and perfection, between partial and imperfect, urging the community to seek perfection *in* the completion. For him, love is the way to achieve perfection in the end.

I recognize and acknowledge the complexity and trickiness Paul encounters when he tries to imagine new and expansive possibilities while using the blurred and myopic lens of his own experiences. He can grasp the notion of an *eschaton* that dismantles the *power* of difference, while simultaneously being beholden to the ways in which those differences are marked on our bodies and personhood. Thus, we ought to pay attention to his (albeit muddled) words, as his talk of love illustrates what it means to call folks in the "here and now" into the perfect end that their *ekklēsia* presupposes.

Love vs. Knowledge

Paul's talk of love theologically responds to the philosophical norms of the Corinthian context, in which knowledge (*sophia*, wisdom) is the highest value.[5] Paul subverts this cultural truth by offering a theological one: love produces full knowledge. Using the symbol of the ἔσοπτρον—speculum/mirror—(apropos since mirrors were a part of the Corinthian industry) as well as the distinction between whole/complete and perfect/imperfect, Paul compares imperfect reflection to face-to-face divine perception. In Corinth, mirrors were made not out of glass but out of shined metal (including steel and bronze), giving the dull/dim/distorted reflection.[6] In the end, however, the (w)hol(l)y perfect view will do away with imperfect human-made technology of knowing (v. 10). Members of the church will not be looking at a reflection of the object of themselves; instead, they will truly perceive one another, without mediation or distortion or enigma. In this exchange of seeing one another, they co-create one another and themselves, not as subjects or objects, but as subject-objects who rest in the vulnerability of being known by the other while being accountable for knowing another. This exchange is the space of love. Even more, this process of co-creation—intersubjective production—is eternal, not belonging entirely to temporality but finding its home there. *This* is why *agape* is both outside and inside space and time; it produces and reproduces our collective existence.

Love is the full realization of seeing and being seen by another. Embedded in this perception is self-sacrifice (as vulnerability), intention (as attention),[7] and revelation (as disclosure). To love and be loved, then, is to participate in the sacred process that God establishes in the Incarnation. It is to make oneself perceptible by and vulnerable to the other. This process requires faith, not simply in God, but in the other's capacity to hold the fullness of who we are, to care for us, to tend our wounds, to work toward and support our full actualization. This process of caring and loving into sight requires not our diminishment but our mutually encouraged flourishing through self-revelation. In this way, the sacrifice of self is not abnegation; rather it is the submission to the possibility of intersubjective simultaneity—being both subject and object in order to be created in and with community. A significant element of Paul's speech in this letter, then, is a plea for folks to participate in the eschatological aim, to be co-creators of one another's humanity. Engaging in this process is to know fully, as one has been known . . . by God.

Love endures beyond the constructs of our understanding, beyond our technologies of vision, beyond machinations of sight. It produces full knowledge and deep perception, and knowing, as Paul describes it, is not about a kind of relationality that is steeped in our loss of our selves. Rather, full knowing is about our capacity and willingness to fully perceive ourselves without the distortion of a dim mirror. Again, to know fully is to know as we have been known—with and through the vulnerability, grace, compassion, and hopefulness that substantiates such love.

REFRACTING THE SPECULUM:
LOVE AS MUTUAL SELF-REVELATION

Love is about the space, effort, and experience of making space for one another and ourselves to exist. It is the process of making, which comes from releasing control. Love gives us the capacity to perceive and reflect ourselves and one another, which is how, arguably, our existence is substantiated. In this way, love is based on the witnessing of our experiences and the response to what we witness. This is why love is something that we both give and receive, the mutual exchange of revelation and attentive perception.

The metaphor of the speculum/mirror was certainly useful in Paul's effort to contextualize his argument, but it was also a tool to illustrate the type of intersubjectivity for which love makes space. Love produces new knowledge through self-revelation, and this is the kind of knowing that comes from a willingness to be known. And this willingness—this *consent*—is key. Luce Irigaray warns us about the dehumanizing effect of non-consensual objectification that can result from the use of a speculum.[8] In a misogynistic patriarchy, the speculum is not a reflective instrument; it is a penetrative one.[9] Using the speculum/mirror as an instrument of power through which one is able to perceive the other, one person has no real regard for the experience of personhood of another. For Irigaray, the speculum cannot be a mirror; it is always a kaleidoscope, rendering the viewed object more an image of speculation than charitable observation. This is why, then, the objects perceived through the speculum remain a mystery to the viewer; the lens (or the opening, as it were) refracts, rather than reveals what is in view. So, then, if a misogynistic patriarchy is the lens, then the real image of the woman (and I would extend this to any oppressed personhood) remains in obscurity.

This is exactly opposite of what Paul suggests will happen in the end. In Paul's estimation, the willingness to be perceived by another is a choice to be present with, rather than set apart from another. The disclosure that happens in this self-revelation is a way of dissolving real (or imagined) boundaries, including the one between the divine and human.[10] This revelation, in bridging human and divine, makes eternity something to which God's creation now has access. Likewise, the possibility of finitude is something that God experiences in the process of revealing God's self through incarnation. Thus, the elimination of the boundary between human and divine is not simply about the human ability to become divine. Rather, it is an illustration of the divine willingness to be human.

I imagine that Paul uses the term *agape* for love because it is God who first illustrates the practice of vulnerability and a holy capacity for self-surrender. Christian ethicist Timothy P. Jackson emphasizes the importance of this illustration in his book, *The Priority of Love: Christian Charity and Social Justice.* Jackson suggests that this love cannot end or begin with human (temporal/ temporary) investments in praise or reward.[11] He argues that because "God *is* love (1 John 4:8), and we are dependent on God's gracious self-revelation for a rudimentary understanding of and participation in this Goodness," then we must remember that any real experience of love begins and ends with God.[12] According to Jackson, *agape* is the love for which humans are made, and it "involves three basic features: (1) unconditional willing of the good for the other, (2) equal regard for the well-being of the other, and (3) passionate service open to self-sacrifice for the sake of the other."[13] We manifest *agape* in our perception of and connection with the other.

Paul is interested in building the ecclesial community, and he recognizes that the enactment of *agape* is the way to make meaning of the spiritual gifts that he lists in Chapter 12 and verses 1–3 of this chapter. Without love, tongues are simply noise. Without love, prophetic powers and deep understanding have no significance.[14] Paul wants the Corinthians to understand how empty such gifts are if they do not work toward the common good. The common good, in case it is unclear, is the intentional creation and re-creation of life. Philosopher and theologian Jean-Luc Marion believes that intentionality is a significant component of such creative and intersubjective work. There is a difference, Marion asserts, between the *I* who intentionally sees and the *me* who is intentionally seen in the process of love.[15] Without intention, our love is merely a projection of that which we experience; it is *our idea* of another.[16] Outside of intention, we do not project our image to another to love, or offer ourselves to be perceived. Instead, we reflect an image of ourselves. This is why Marion references the mirror. For him, this is a phenomenological issue of self-idolatry: unintentioned love is self-love. To really perceive one another, rather than project abstractions of our inter-pretations of another, we must "render [ourselves] there in an unconditional surrender. . . . No other gaze must respond to the ecstasy of *this particular* other exposed in [our] gaze."[17] Such a surrender is what Paul means by see-ing face to face.

Once we have fully perceived one another, which is really about making space for ourselves and another to truly *be*, then we can truly exist in com-munity with one another. This is why being a self that can be fully known is an ethical process. It involves the creation of self and other through a mutual practice of gentleness that does not require an erasure of the self, but that does require responsibility for another.[18] It is in this responsibility that we find our humanity. Echoing Paul's main ideas about ethical community, eter-nal things, intersubjectivity, as well as Simone Weil's attention, Emmanuel Levinas explains it this way:

> It is only in approaching the Other that I attend to myself. This does not mean that my existence is constituted in the thought of the others. . . . The face I wel-come makes me pass from phenomenon to being in another sense: . . . I expose myself to the questioning of the Other, and this urgency of the response—acuteness of the present—engenders me for responsibility; as responsible I am brought to my final reality. This extreme attention does not actualize what was in potency, for it is not conceivable without the other. Being attentive signifies a surplus of consciousness, and presupposes the call of the other. To be atten-tive is to recognize the mastery of the other, to receive his command, or, more exactly, to receive from him the command to command. When I seek my final reality, I find that my existence as a "thing in itself" begins with the presence in me of the idea of Infinity. But this relation consists in serving the Other.[19]

To be clear, knowledge is secondary to the ethical duty of responsibility for the other. More important for Levinas—and Paul, for that matter—is the eternal preservation of the whole. Such preservation sustains individual subjects. According to John S. Mbiti, "The existence of the individual is the existence of the corporate."[20] Hence, we have Mbiti's most famous aphorism, "I am because we are,"[21] which stands in contrast to Descartes' "I think, therefore I am."[22]

When I conducted research on black queer families in 2010, one of my research participants offered a reflection that I find useful in relation to Paul's delineation of the differences between love and knowing, and also in relation to the ethical process of really attending to the other that Weil, Levinas, and Marion articulate. Harriet said, "I think that the whole lesbian thing is a very creative expression of existence and loving each other, and I think it also speaks to a level of what I believe to be the infinite quality of love because you can never—I do believe this, that you can love someone all your life and never reach the boundaries of who they are as a person."[23] Harriet's words illustrate the limits of knowledge through love, and she seems to say that such a limit actually produces freedom. It frees us from categorical, behavioral, and structural norms and allows us to love one another without the constrictions and restrictions of mediation.

Such unrestricted love results from mutual investments in our own and another's freedom. According to Episcopal priest and theologian Carter Heyward, "mutuality is the process by which we create and liberate one another."[24] In Corinth, Paul is calling for a revolutionary set of relationships that are mutually liberating and underwritten by accountability. He wants the Corinthians to be loved for who they really are, or as Heyward puts it, as their "least hidden and most spontaneous selves."[25] This process requires mutual honesty, presence, and vulnerability. Additionally, creation and liberation signal the sacred process of relational empowerment "because it brings us into embodied realization of ourselves in relation."[26] Heyward further argues:

> If we do not live even partially in the sacred realm of right relation, so stuck are we in the fear of mutuality and its consequence. . . . To live through these dynamics of alienated power toward the realization of our power in right relation is not merely to focus, however, on 'last things. . . .' To the contrary, our power draws us into our own beginnings . . . into our relatedness. Here, we participate in liberating one another from the isolation, brokenness, and despair wrought by abusive power relations in the great and small place of our lives.[27]

For Heyward, these mutual relations of power are how we are able to experience God as love.[28] This love comes from God and thus belongs to God; yet, when it moves among us and when we embody and express it, that love becomes ours as well.[29]

CONCLUSION: DIVINE EROTIC LOVE

If, as Marion suggest, we "love only through the lived experiences of our consciousness," then we ought to ask ourselves by what means those lived experiences become known to us.[30] For Heyward, it is our shared experience of relational power, felt through our senses, that allows us to know ourselves, our lover(s), and God. The *experience* and *sense* of love are the root of a theological epistemology.[31] God is found in the erotic, in the messiness of human experience and mutual self-revelation. Love requires the highly vulnerable risk of reaching out to others and allowing ourselves to be touched, held, supported, and protected by them.[32]

And yet, within a white supremacist ableist cis-heteropatriarchy, it is hard to imagine such a sharing of power through vulnerability and submission to another. Feminists, womanists, and scholars of queer religion/theology have been right to push back against any notion of love as self-sacrifice because within such a context, that move is about relinquishing agency to oppressive authority and hegemonic forces. Fortunately, Heyward helps us read Paul's emphasis on love in a different way. She turns the notion of self-sacrifice on its head: rather than loss, self-sacrificial love is about releasing the sole responsibility of one's own wellbeing. In short, self-sacrifice is not about what or for whom we are willing to die. Instead, it is about what and for whom we are willing to truly live. This kind of living requires a commitment to relational life, to accountability, to caring for others' wounds and allowing our wounds to be tended to as well. This mutual self-revelation is a sacred trust, not merely for a redemptive hereafter, but in the realization of an accountable community right now.

Paul's special offering to the Corinthians is the truth that they can access this divine love right now, in community with one another. Even more, he reveals that *agape depends* on erotic knowing. When Paul describes love's virtues, he depends on his experiences. "Love is patient; love is kind; love is not envious or boastful or arrogant or rude."[33] How does one experience or acknowledge kindness except through one's experience and sense of it? Kindness is felt on the body, in our skin, in our touch and taste. We see and hear it. We *sense* it. Moreover, how does love avoid "insist[ing] on its own way," or irritability and resentfulness?[34] Love makes itself known through our bodies and feelings. Paul expects the Corinthians—and us—to trust those experiences of *agape* so that we can distinguish it from lesser gifts.

This internal trust is what black lesbian feminist poet Audre Lorde calls forth from us—not a turning away from our erotic knowledge but a turning inward and toward one another. Lorde notes, "To refuse to be conscious of what we are feeling at any time, however comfortable that might seem, is to deny a large part of the experience, and to allow ourselves to be reduced to the pornographic, the abused, and the absurd."[35] This distortion of the erotic's power reinforces docility, obedience, and external definition—all of which contribute to the cycle of oppression through the process of dehumanization.[36] For Lorde, the erotic is an *episteme*, a means by which we can attain excellence. In her estimation, the liberating power of the erotic begins with the self, and she laments the fact that people—especially women—have been taught "to suspect what is deepest in ourselves."[37] Lorde helps me read Paul as a supporter of erotic love, since he advocates for divine knowledge through the Corinthians' senses and experiences of one another.

Heyward co-signs Lorde and simultaneously uses her ideas theologically, suggesting that "if we learn to trust our senses, our capacities to touch, taste, smell, hear, see, and thereby know, they can teach us what is good and what is bad, what is real and what is false, for us in relation to one another and to the earth and cosmos."[38] Lorde claims that this knowledge is deeply empowering and states, "our erotic knowledge empowers us, becomes a lens through which we scrutinize all aspects of our existence."[39] This lens lacks mediation. It is the face-to-face experience that Paul promises. Such a lens does not allow us to ignore, erase, or marginalize one another; nor does it promote harm or dehumanization. Paul's plea for a face-to-face love is an investment in a social ethic that, were we to heed it, would insure our collective survival in the end and, more importantly, right now.

ROUNDTABLE CONVERSATION

1. Manifest Love

Jacob: I'd like to start us off by naming something that you perform in your essay, Nikki. Throughout this book, we've been thinking about the *particularities* of our speech, especially, how our ways of speaking are situated in specific ethnic/racial, gendered, and sex/ual ways of being. We saw this first in Eric's opening chapter on Spirit Speech, where he situated God-talk not in some universally translatable patois but in particular-communal ways of thinking and speaking. Here near the end of our book, you open your reflections on love out of the emotional and material blessings of your community, and particularly with your mother—may she rest in peace. I wonder if you can help us reflect more on what you label the "tangible manifestations of love."

Nikki: Love, and the speech that arises out of it, must be manifested as *eros*. It must be felt. This is why I want to help us think about Paul's discourse on *agape* as an effort to establish room for an *eros* he wants to be manifested in the community at Corinth. In other words, *eros* is the means by which we see, feel, and understand *agape*. It makes sense to me that we may speak of eternity and universality only in relation to the ways that we think about and attend to material realities.

Eric: You two know how much I tend to reject binaries. (Chuckles). I appreciate the way that you are troubling the simple opposition between *agápe* and *erōs*. As you allow these modes or expressions or notions of love to speak to one another, other dualities begin to falter—the very dualities that are causing the Corinthians so much conflict. When we challenge the simple opposition between time and eternity, particularity and universality, body and spirit, self and community, etc. we're performing acts of love: a transgressive love.

Jacob: Well spotted, Eric! I think that it's important here to unpack what we mean by *erōs*. When most folks think about the erotic, they think of something that is associated with sex, maybe even in a sordid way. But that's not what we're talking about, is it?

Nikki: Absolutely not! We must set erotic love in opposition to any mode of relation that objectifies others. Pornography, for instance, is the antithesis of love because it radically reduces the other to an object of desire; it turns the other into a *thing* (Lorde). Above all, love preserves the other as subject.

Eric: At base, love refuses to harm the other, as Paul will argue. It is not selfish. It does not use the other for one's own ends. As such, it protects the unique otherness of the other. It approaches the other barefooted, because the space love opens between the self and the other is holy ground. Even as love is driven by a desire to be in relation with the other, it is halted by care for the other, which refuses to reduce the other's alterity.

2. Transgressive Love

Nikki: This is a very important part of my work. As I mention in my essay, as a black queer ethicist, one of the things that I look for when reading any text (and especially biblical texts) is whether or not the writer (or speaker in the text) is using language to reinforce injustice and hegemonic forces or to subvert and resist them. New Testament scholars differ in their interpretations of what exactly Paul is up to here. I find merit in many of these approaches, and I argue that Paul is calling for a nuanced view of love that works against established norms and social scripts by deconstructing the Corinthian hierarchies altogether.

Eric: This makes me wonder about the temporal dimensions of transgressive love. You highlight two ways that you see Paul speaking about the future. How might the transgressive love you identify in 1 Cor. 13 play between *telōs* and *eschaton*? In other words, I'm interested in hearing you speak further about the contrast between the temporal and the eternal. It seems to me that if we have access to something beyond, it's always through the incarnational moment, i.e., particularity.

Nikki: Temporality arises out of engagement, namely, in seeing individuals. Thus, the eternal is tied to the communal. In drawing a distinction between *telos* (the end) and *eschaton* (the goal), Paul can grasp the notion of an eschaton that dismantles the *power* of difference, while simultaneously being beholden to the ways in which those differences are marked on our bodies and personhood. Thus, we ought to pay attention to his (albeit muddled) words, as his talk of love illustrates what it means to call folks in the "here and now" into the perfect end that their *ekklēsia* presupposes.

Jacob: I like how you are leading us to interrogate the epistemological underpinnings of Paul's rhetoric here, Nikki. Commenting on this pericope, Margaret Mitchell has argued that "love is the mortar between the bricks of the Christian building." I contend that Paul's thinking here is less like mortar and more like dynamite. Paul is advancing an alternative epistemology for the believer that destabilizes the Greco-Roman status quo. His speech, along with the love his speech calls for, *must* be transgressive or we will remain unaware to the material and existential particularities of the *ekklēsia*.

3. The Force of Sight

Eric: I'm glad that you brought up awareness and to what we bear witness, Jake. So much of this book has focused on discourse—ways of speaking and hearing that are all too often delimited by our ways of thinking. Let's talk a bit about the interplay between mirror and actual sight. There's something we can see but also a "force" that allows us to see something more. In other words, while attention to the particularities of another are vital to a kind of erotic encounter (in the sense of erotic that we've been discussing), the Spirit also enables us to see something else, something more.

Jacob: Let me add to this point, Eric, by challenging us to also think about the relation between the *force* of sight and a certain *fore*sight that obtains between the face-to-face encounter and the specular/imperfect perception of the self. I'm intrigued by Nikki's mention of how seeing in Corinth maps onto their technological and economic relationality. Nikki, can you bring the temporality of seeing into this discussion to help us to parse Paul's distinction between *telōs* and *eschaton*?

Nikki: Sure. Members of the eschatological Church will not be looking at a mere reflection of themselves when they attend to the other; instead, they will truly perceive one another, without mediation or distortion or enigma. In this exchange of seeing one another, they co-create one another and themselves— not as subjects or objects but as subject-objects—who rest in the vulnerability of being known by the other while being accountable for knowing another. This exchange is the space of love. Even more, this process of co-creation (or inter-subjective production) is eternal.

Jacob: Might we call this, to borrow from Charles Taylor, an *erotic social imaginary*? If this is close to what Paul is getting at here in 1 Cor. 13—and I think he is—it ties in with that "something more" that you mentioned a moment ago, *Eric:* a way of seeing at once in and beyond material phenomena that's only possible when enabled by the Spirit.

Nikki, you rightly note the importance of 1 Cor. 12:31 for understanding what Paul is saying in chapter 13. Richard Horsley notes both the irony and the translational difficulties of this transitional verse, which hinges both Paul's discussion of spiritual gifts that precedes it and his epistemological deliberations that follow. The adverbial Greek idiom *kath' hyperbolēn* is frequently rendered adjectivally (e.g., NRSV) as modifying a certain *way* (*hodos*): in short, a "still more excellent way." Horsley renders the feminine noun as a verb ("Strive, even exceedingly, for the greater gifts. I will show you a way."). This moves us further but not far enough. I read the noun *hyperbolēn* as a noun and the adverb *kata* as an adverb of direction (which is most common in the accusative case), and I suggest we read the verse thusly: "And now I will show you a way toward superabundance." It is not the way itself that is exceeding or superabundant; rather, an erotic approach opens a new path. Hereby, we are able to discern that which is given (i.e., the material realities others experience) in a different frame. What is then received in this way gives itself to us beyond the capacities of our cultural-linguistic epistemologies (i.e., superabundance).

4. The Epistemology of Love

Nikki: Here is where the difference of personhood really comes to the fore.

Eric: Nikki, you note that Paul's "bridge" is *self*-revelation. Should we clarify for our readers that *self*-revelation is always already tied to the communal? Self-revelation smacks of "I think, therefore I am."

Jacob: What would be illuminating for readers is for you to say it as you did and then create space for us to name the point of confusion. It's in the coming to awareness of how these terms (i.e., "self" and "revelation") have their own history and heritage that we don't choose. You can't ever reject that heritage without first seeing it as a heritage.

Eric: Yes so when I read "self," I think less about what I would read than the way that others readers might assume the turn inward rather than an engagement in community. So, is there a way to turn the self toward community at the outset so that folks don't miss the later move toward community?

Jacob: It was through my engagement with Jean-Luc Marion's work (among others) that I realized that the Cartesian elevation of the self as the center of knowledge makes it structurally impossible for us to love God and neighbor. We can't love God, self, or other as long as we turn each other into objects.

Nikki: God is found in the erotic, in the messiness of human experience and mutual self-revelation. Love requires the highly vulnerable risk of reaching out to others and allowing ourselves to be touched, held, supported, and protected by them. Plus, an absence of words is not an accident. I think that we lose the opportunities to articulate points of identitarian confusion, especially if we are navigating dominant culture as people who have access to and use dominant discourse. We, people who are marginalized, tend to be bilingual; both languages come to us seemingly naturally. We are code switching and using double consciousness. Remember, we do, in fact, "wear the mask" (Paul Laurence Dunbar).

Jacob: I can go to a Greek or German text and pretty much read it because I've learned the language. This is a sign of the virtue of the education I've received and the people who have exposed me to these other ways of thinking and being. I didn't need to learn to code switch or be bilingual growing up because of my privilege; my education has taught me to be bilingual, in a sense, because I can now recognize the truthfulness of perspectives emerging from different spaces than my own.

Eric: Growing up in mostly white communities like I did, I just had to figure out how to make it work, how to move linguistically and culturally between very different spaces. You also figure out how to center the kind of knowledge most needed in any particular space. This is still true for me; my identity still requires me to function in and in between linguistic and cultural spaces. I've realized though that these skills are not just burdens to carry but assets in the theological work I do. They help me perceive insights I couldn't have otherwise, *and* they help me share those insights in divergent cultural spaces.

Nikki: There is something to be said about the languages that are most easily captured and become respected. The perspective you two had seemed foreign to me because I am so steeped in queer theology and philosophy; five years ago, it would have struck me. Yes, you are bilingual. It's like me looking at Japanese characters, and I can't make any sense of it. But a language with Roman letters is something I can make out in some way.

Jacob: It wasn't in theology courses that I was struck with the strangeness of the discursive frame you are describing, Nikki. It was not until I took a feminist philosophy course that I encountered some of the concepts that inform you essay. I was struck in that class by how foreign these ideas sounded, but for everyone else in the class (or so it seemed), this stuff was old hat! I was in a room where everyone spoke in a kind of different language. It was disorienting to be expected to make meaning as they did. This opened up a whole other world of thinking that can tend to be left to the side—even in a robust theological education.

Nikki: What an interesting space in which to learn that stuff. On one hand, I'm sure it was tough, as those feminist philosophy students probably didn't allow you to get away with much. On the other hand, what a comfortable and sanitized experience it must have been to learn this material in a space (and body) in which you don't have to worry about being the object of someone's gaze or placed in a physically, socially, or psychologically vulnerable position.

NOTES

1. Nikki Young's Facebook page, accessed May 28, 2017, https://www.facebook.com/nikki.young.902.
2. This is a reference to Paul's speech in Ephesians 3. From his imprisoned position, Paul echoes in this letter a theme that he introduces in 1 Corinthians: God's love creates fuller understanding of ourselves and one another while also providing grace, generosity, and care. See specifically verses 18–19, "I pray that you may have the power to comprehend, with all the saints, what is the breadth and length and height and depth, and to know the love of Christ that surpasses knowledge, so that you may be filled with all the fullness of God" (NRSV).
3. Elisabeth Schüssler Fiorenza, "1 Corinthians," in *HarperCollins Bible Commentary*, revised edition, ed. James L. Mays (New York: HarperCollins, 2000), 1074–75.
4. Here, I use "common good" to describe the survival and flourishing of this small community within the environs of Corinth. Though Paul's vision of the Body of Christ eventually extends beyond small communities, his primary interests seem to lie with the burgeoning church in Corinth.
5. Schüssler Fiorenza, "1 Corinthians," 1074.
6. Ibid.
7. Here, I am drawing on Simone Weil's concept of attention. For her, attention is concerned with understanding—without cloudiness or self-blocking mediation—what the other is experiencing. Inasmuch as it calls for our willingness to be open to the other, this process fosters the virtue of humility. It also reminds the attentive person(s) that we are bearing witness to the reality of one another's existence. Weil points to the ways in which purposeful attention is concerned with understanding—without cloudiness or self-blocking mediation—what the other is experiencing. For her, this process helps one to acquire the virtue of humility and reminds the attentive listener that she is bearing witness to the fact that the storyteller and her reality exist. Simone Weil, *Waiting for God* (New York: Perennial Classics, 2001), 59.
8. Luce Irigaray, *Speculum of the Other Woman*, trans. Gillian C. Gill (Ithaca, NY: Cornell University Press, 1985), 133.
9. Ibid.
10. Patrick Cheng discusses this at length, arguing that God's own revelation—God's "coming out"—is the perfect example of radical love. Revealing God's self through scripture, reason, and the incarnation, God sends forth love in the process.

Such a love dissolves boundaries between the divine and human and divine, powerful and weak, and knowing and unknowing. See *Radical Love: An Introduction to Queer Theology* (New York: Seabury Books, 2011), 43–55.

11. Timothy P. Jackson, *The Priority of Love: Christian Charity and Social Justice* (Princeton, NJ: Princeton University Press, 2003), 5.

12. Ibid., 8.

13. Ibid., 10.

14. 1 Cor. 13:1–3 (NRSV)

15. Jean-Luc Marion, *Prolegomena to Charity*, trans. Stephen E. Lewis (New York: Fordham University Press, 2002), 77–78.

16. Ibid., 74–76.

17. Ibid., 101.

18. Emmanuel Levinas, *Totality and Infinity: An Essay on Exteriority*, trans. Alphonso Lingis (Pittsburgh, PA: Duquesne University Press, 1969), 178.

19. Ibid., 178–79.

20. John S. Mbiti, *African Religions and Philosophy*, 2nd ed. (Portsmouth, NH: Heinemann, 1990), 141.

21. Ibid., 106.

22. René Descartes, *Discourse on Method of Rightly Conducting the Reason and Seeking the Truth in the Sciences*, Vol. XXXIV, Part 1, The Harvard Classics (New York: P.F. Collier & Son, 1909–1914), 27.

23. Harriett Tubman (pseudo.), interview by the author, field notes, Atlanta, GA, 3 May 2010. She chose this pseudonym to represent the way that living into her identity as a legally blind, black lesbian is like traversing the underground of our society and leading people through darkness to places of freedom, renewal, and safety.

24. Carter Heyward, *Touching Our Strength: The Erotic as Power and the Love of God* (San Francisco: Harper and Row Publishers, 1989), 105.

25. Ibid., 107.

26. Ibid., 91.

27. Ibid., 92.

28. Ibid., 99.

29. Ibid.

30. Marion, *Prolegomena*, 74.

31. Heyward, *Touching Our Strength*, 99.

32. Ibid., 100.

33. 1 Cor. 13:4–5 (NRSV).

34. 1 Cor. 13:5 (NRSV).

35. Audre Lorde, "Uses of the Erotic: The Erotic as Power," in *Sister Outsider: Speeches and Essays,* rev. ed. (New York: Crown Publishing, 2007), 59.

36. Ibid., 58.

37. Audre Lorde and Adrienne Rich, "An Interview with Audre Lorde," *Signs* 4, no. 6 (1981): 730.

38. Heyward, *Touching Our Strength*, 93.

39. Lorde, "Uses of the Erotic," 57.

Roundtable Conclusion

1. Processing

Eric: Reflecting on *how* we produced this work, I'm struck by the process that got us here. First, we wrote separately; we did the scholarly work we do all the time. But then, we dialogued virtually. We met via Skype or FaceTime or whatever technology was not crashing the Internet at the moment. We spent time on each other's writing, pressing on points of disagreement as well as wondering about and celebrating moments of insight and new clarity. Last, we gathered together in the same place to see each other in person, to feel our presence in the room, to hear one another without the mediation of a computer. We also ate together and played together. Not surprisingly, we played a board game centered on pathways and moving from one place to another. Something happened in those various encounters.

Jacob: When I approached you two about this book, I feared that no press would touch it because it seemed so nebulous. And, I didn't know if it would be a train wreck. What I loved about our process was that we trained ourselves to guard against the risk of misspeaking. Buttressed by our friendship and common purpose, we embraced the challenges each other offered to our respective essays.

Nikki: I think *that* training breathed life into this project in a special way, especially because the fear that you mention tends to keep people divided—segregated—and has locked many of us into limited modes of discourse. What we are doing in this book and through our collaborative process is bearing witness to a mystery that we have seen and heard in our engagement together. It's not a joke. This is what could really happen. This is, frankly, something like what Paul seems to have been talking about in 1 Corinthians. I hope that people catch the ways that we were present with one another and notice something beyond an awesome set of methodological skills on display.

I also want to name that we worked with one another using spoken and un-spoken elements of critical generosity.[1] Ours was a work of seeing and being seen, offering interventions and endeavoring to really take on what one another tried to communicate. In this way, we became one another's dramaturgs, offer-ing explanations and renderings of each other's work in ways that drew out our individual and collective voices and held each one of us accountable . . . at least to ourselves. That is, we invited one another to really face what we had written and spoken about the text, to be present with our claims in a way that allowed them not to be "challenged" but to be curated into honest reflections of our full selves. At moments, this process might have felt solely critical, calling for one or all of us to think or feel again the words we offered; most times, though, our process was riddled with the simultaneity of critique and generativity.

2. Identity

Jacob: One of the things we worked on quite intentionally in our engage-ment with these texts and with one another is our cultural particularities. We leaned into the play of sameness and otherness that marks each of our self-understandings. But, even as we strove to attend to one another's differences, there are also commonalities that perhaps mark the very possibility of this kind and quality of discussion.

Eric: I think that's right. At the very least, we shared some core political and theological commitments that made our conversations generative. As we outline in the preface, certain events stirred in us a sense that we had to respond, that we had to resist the encroachments of oppressive forces in our world today. I think we shared a commitment that the everyday stuff of human existence is not de-tachable from theological and political reflection but its very essence. If we were going to say something about speaking *about* and *with* God, then we had to speak into the realities on the ground we see and experience. It wouldn't be enough to remain in some realm of theory; we had to say something that mattered.

Nikki: I think we started by noting that WE matter. As individuals with roots that converge and complement, conflict and complicate one another's lives and histories, we remained grounded in the idea and practice of our collective significance. I think that some of that came from our shared identity as alums of Emory's GDR. Our Emory heritage gave us the core pedagogical conviction of interdisciplinarity. Our professors and colleagues taught us to be respectful and generous and appreciative of various scholarly perspectives. We practiced this in our engagement with one another. We knew that doing this kind of work called for the simultaneity of intersectionality and interdisciplinarity. And, thankfully, we committed to it.

Jacob: Is there, then, a kind of lowest common denominator necessary for this kind of work? In other words, must we hold certain values or identity markers in common for conversations like this to take place with and among others?

Eric: I wonder about that. Might we say that the prerequisite for generative theological work is not agreement on all the particulars so much as a common commitment to the flourishing of others? After all, I felt that as we worked more and more together, a great deal of serendipity emerged. I mean it this way: the more we read each other's stuff, the more it felt like we could write in one another's voices. But that's not exactly right because we are our own people. Yet, sometimes, our voices came together, especially as we edited and revised one another's words. New mysteries and questions opened up to make us interested in what each of us had to contribute. But more than anything else, we were committed that each of our voices could be heard clearly, loudly, authentically.

Nikki: There is a difference between revising and editing one another's work and making room for our collective speech. We didn't always know how to do it, and we struggled with considering the implications of the difference. It is possible that our experience in writing together parallels the process that each of us experienced when we encountered the text.

Jacob: Reading isn't just about learning about the other; it's about taking on another's language a bit. I think that this insight came from our engagement with Eric's essay on Pentecost. The disciples were "together in one place." They shared breath, and in that sharing the Spirit expanded their discursive possibilities. Perhaps each of us speaks—in tongues of mortals and angels—with an accent. We learn to speak out of particular cultural contexts and these cultures inflect our ways of thinking, speaking, and relating in distinct ways.

3. Writing in the Last Days

Nikki: I am so glad that we committed some time to write together in person. Being face-to-face with one another was different than writing separately or even writing together through the mediation of a computer screen. We noticed and responded to one another's facial micro movements, tonal inflections, and shifts in posture. We learned about how each of us takes in and processes information. We gave grace-filled moments of pause for each of us to let things sink in. We allowed one another to have shifts in thought and come back again to ideas that we laid aside.

Ours was a sense-driven process. We perceived and learned from one another using all of our senses. We hugged, we ate, played, we anticipated desserts . . . we got drenched in a rainstorm. We were present in body, and we finished this book using every bit of ourselves.

Eric: There was a "something else," "something more" that emerged in our conversations. That something else brought increased clarity, certainly, but even more a deeper relationality. We shared stories that never made it on the pages of the book but indelibly marked what we wrote and how we wrote alongside one another. Might we dare to say that that something else, that something more is the moving of the Spirit? Is that one way to discern the presence of God, when we sense and feel and embody connection and possibility?

Jacob: And we wrote the hell out of this book! Seriously, I've never had a more generative and productive writing retreat. We accomplished more in two days than I believe any of us could have on our own. What does it say about our institutions? Scholarship and sermon writing are too often isolated from real people (other than the author). I wonder if that is why some of us struggle at times to generate content for the life and work of the church.

4. Moving Forward

Jacob: So, where do we go from here? How can this work and experience together inform our future work (together)?

Nikki: Book tour, anyone? Let's evangelize! Or, in a less forceful and pedantic way (winks at Jacob), let's be open to talking about speaking in new tongues. That is, maybe we can be open to further conversations about the bold, spirit and love-filled, speech that anyone makes possible when attending to the matter of the day.

Eric: (Chuckles) Think about all the frequent flyer miles we could collect! In all seriousness, though, I will be interested to hear how our work might make a difference to students, scholars, and practitioners. It's always the surprising, unexpected results that bring me most joy. I never would have thought someone would be motivated to do a certain thing, but the book opened up that possibility. It's part of the teacher's vocation to be delighted by the unexpected and rich ways our teaching makes a difference.

NOTE

1. Jill Dolan, *The Feminist Spectator in Action: Feminist Criticism for the Stage and Screen* (New York: Palgrave Macmillan, 2013). To read Dolan's inspiration for the concept of critical generosity, see also David Román, *Acts of Intervention: Performance, Gay Culture, and AIDS* (Bloomington: Indiana University Press, 1998).

Bibliography

Ahmed, Sara. "Making Feminist Points." feministkilljoys (blog), September 11, 2013. https://feministkilljoys.com/2013/09/11/making-feminist-points/.

Anderson, Carol. *White Rage: The Unspoken Truth of Our Racial Divide.* New York: Bloomsbury, 2016.

Augustine. *On the Trinity: Books 8–15.* Edited by Gareth B. Matthews. Translated by Stephen McKenna. Cambridge: Cambridge University Press, 2002.

Bade, Rachael, and Burgess Everett. "Why Ryan and McConnell Split over Trump." *Politico.* Last modified October 12, 2016. http://www.politico.com/story/2016/10/paul-ryan-mitch-mcconnell-donald-trump-229629.

Barclay, John M. G. "Crucifixion as Wisdom: Exploring the Ideology of a Disreputable Social Movement." In *The Wisdom and Foolishness of God: First Corinthians 1–2 in Theological Exploration,* edited by Christophe Chalamet and Hans-Christoph Askani, 1–21. Minneapolis: Fortress Press, 2015.

———. *Paul and the Gift.* Grand Rapids: Eerdmans, 2017.

Barreto, Eric D. *Ethnic Negotiations: The Function of Race and Ethnicity in Acts 16.* WUNT II 294. Tübingen: Mohr Siebeck, 2010.

Barrett, C. K. *Acts: A Shorter Commentary.* New York: T & T Clark, 2002.

Bass, Diana Butler. *Christianity after Religion: The End of Church and the Birth of a New Spiritual Awakening.* New York: HarperOne, 2012.

———. *Grounded: Finding God in the World—A Spiritual Revolution.* New York: HarperOne, 2015.

Blass, Friedrich, Albert Debrunner, and Robert W. Funk. *A Greek Grammar of the New Testament and Other Early Christian Literature.* Chicago: University of Chicago Press, 1961.

Brawley, Robert L. "The God of Promises and the Jews in Luke-Acts." In *Literary Studies in Acts: Essays in Honor of Joseph B. Tyson,* edited by Richard P. Thompson and Thomas E. Phillips, 279–96. Macon, GA: Mercer University Press, 1998.

Bruce, F. F. *The Acts of the Apostles: The Greek Text with Introduction and Commentary.* Grand Rapids: Eerdmans, 1990.

116	*Bibliography*

Bullmore, Michael A. *St. Paul's Theology of Rhetorical Style: An Examination of 1 Corinthians 2:1–5 in the Light of First Century Graeco-Roman Rhetorical Culture.* San Francisco: International Scholars Publications, 1995.

Cheng, Patrick. *Radical Love: An Introduction to Queer Theology.* New York: Seabury Books, 2011.

Conzelmann, Hans. "The Address of Paul on the Areopagus." In *Studies in Luke-Acts*, edited by L. E. Keck and J. L. Martyn, 217–30. Mifflintown, PA: Sigler Press, 1980.

———. *A Commentary on the Acts of the Apostles.* Hermeneia. Translated by James Limburg, A. Thomas Kraabel, and Donald H. Juel. Minneapolis: Fortress Press, 1987.

———. *1 Corinthians: A Commentary.* Hermeneia. Translated by James W. Leitch. Philadelphia: Fortress Press, 1975.

Deleuze, Gilles. *Foucault.* Edited and translated by Seán Hand. London: Continuum, 2006.

Derrida, Jacques. "Désistance." In *Psyche: Inventions of the Other, Volume II*, edited by Peggy Kamuf and Elizabeth Rottenberg, translated by Christopher Fynsk, 196–230. Stanford: Stanford University Press, 2008.

———. "The Eyes of Language: The Abyss and the Volcano." In *Acts of Religion*, edited and translated by Gil Anidjar, 189–227. New York: Routledge, 2002.

———. *The Gift of Death; and Literature in Secret.* 2nd edition. Translated by David Wills. Chicago: The University of Chicago Press, 2008.

———. *Given Time: I. Counterfeit Money.* Translated by Peggy Kamuf. Chicago: The University of Chicago Press, 1992.

———. "How to Avoid Speaking: Denials." In *Derrida and Negative Theology*, edited by Harold Coward and Toby Foshay, 73–142. Albany: State University of New York Press, 1992.

———. *Margins of Philosophy.* Translated by Alan Bass. Chicago: The University of Chicago Press, 1982.

———. *Monolinguism of the Other; or, The Prosthesis of Origin.* Translated by Patrick Mensah. Stanford: Stanford University Press, 1998.

———. "A Number of Yes." In *Psyche: Inventions of the Other, Volume II*, edited by Peggy Kamuf and Elizabeth Rottenberg, translated by Brian Holmes, 238–39. Stanford: Stanford University Press, 2008.

———. *Of Grammatology.* Translated by Gayatri Chakravorty Spivak. Corrected edition. Baltimore: The Johns Hopkins University Press, 1976.

———. "Passions: "An Oblique Offering." In *On the Name*, edited by Thomas Dutoit, translated by David Wood, 231–40. Stanford: Stanford University Press, 1995.

———. *Positions.* Translated by Alan Bass. Chicago: The University of Chicago Press, 1981.

———. *Specters of Marx: The State of the Debt, the Work of Mourning and the New International.* Translated by Peggy Kamuf. New York: Routledge, 1994.

———. *Speech and Phenomenon: And Other Essays on Husserl's Theory of Signs.* Translated by Dale B. Alison. Evanston, IL: Northwestern University Press, 1973.

———. "The Time Is Out of Joint." In *Deconstruction Is/In America: A New Sense of the Political*, edited by Anselm Havercamp, 14–39. New York: New York University Press, 1995.

Descartes, René. *Discourse on Method of Rightly Conducting the Reason and Seeking the Truth in the Sciences*. Vol. XXXIV, Part 1, The Harvard Classics. New York: P.F. Collier and Son, 1909–1914.

———. "Third Meditation." In *Meditations on First Philosophy: With Selections from the Objections and Replies*, edited and translated by John Cottingham, 24–36. Cambridge: Cambridge University Press, 1996.

Dolan, Jill. *The Feminist Spectator in Action: Feminist Criticism for the Stage and Screen*. New York: Palgrave Macmillan, 2013.

Duckworth, Jessicah Krey. *Wide Welcome: How the Unsettling Presence of Newcomers Can Save the Church*. Minneapolis: Fortress, 2013.

Dunn, James D. G. *The Acts of the Apostles*. Valley Forge: Trinity Press International, 1996.

Elliott, Neil. "The Apostle Paul and Empire." In *In the Shadow of Empire: Reclaiming the Bible as a History of Faithful Resistance*, edited by Richard A. Horsley, 97–116. Louisville: Westminster John Knox, 2008.

———. *The Arrogance of Nations: Reading Romans in the Shadow of Empire*. Paul in Critical Contexts. Minneapolis: Fortress, 2008.

Feldman, Louis H. *Jew and Gentile in the Ancient World: Attitudes and Interactions from Alexander to Justinian*. Princeton: Princeton University Press, 1993.

Fiore, Benjamin. "The Hortatory Function of Paul's Boasting." *Proceedings* 5 (1985): 39–46.

Fiorenza, Elisabeth Schüssler. "1 Corinthians." In *HarperCollins Bible Commentary*, rev. ed., edited by James L. Mays, 1168–89. San Francisco: Harper and Row, 2000.

Fitzmyer, Joseph A. *The Acts of the Apostles*. Anchor Bible 31. New York: Doubleday, 1998.

Foucault, Michel. "Discourse and Truth: The Problematization of *Parrhesia*." Lecture 6, accessed November 13, 2016. http://foucault.info/documents/parrhesia/.

———. *History of Madness*. Edited by Jean Khalfa. Translated by Jonathan Murphy. London: Routledge, 2006.

———. "History of Systems of Thought." In *Language, Counter-Memory, Practice: Selected Essays and Interviews*, edited by Donald F. Bouchard, translated by Donald F. Bouchard and Sherry Simon, 199–204. Ithaca, NY: Cornell University Press, 1977.

———. *Lectures on the Will to Know: Lectures at the Collège de France, 1970–1971*. Edited by Daniel Defert. Translated by Graham Burchell. New York: Palgrave Macmillan, 2013.

———. *The Order of Things: An Archeology of the Human Sciences*. New York: Vintage Books, 1994.

———. "A Preface to Transgression." In *Language, Counter-Memory, Practice: Selected Essays and Interviews*, edited by Donald F. Bouchard, translated by Donald F. Bouchard and Sherry Simon, 29–52. Ithaca: Cornell University Press, 1977.

———. *"Society Must Be Defended": Lectures at the Collége de France, 1975–1976*. Edited by Arnold I. Davidson. Translated by David Macey. New York: Picador, 2003.

———. "Space, Knowledge, and Power." In *The Foucault Reader*, edited by Paul Rabinow, 239–56. New York: Pantheon Books, 1984.

———. "Truth and Power." In *The Foucault Reader*, edited by Paul Rabinow, 51–75. New York: Pantheon Books, 1984.

Given, Mark D. "Not Either/or but Both/and in Paul's Areopagus Speech." *Biblical Interpretation* 3 (1995): 356–72.

Glaude, Eddie S., Jr. *Democracy in Black: How Race Still Enslaves the American Soul*. New York: Crown, 2016.

Haenchen, Ernst. *The Acts of the Apostles: A Commentary*. Translated by Bernard Noble and Gerald Shinn. Philadelphia: Westminster, 1971.

Hays, Richard B. *Echoes of Scripture in the Letters of Paul*. New Haven: Yale University Press, 1989.

Heyward, Carter. *Touching Our Strength: The Erotic as Power and the Love of God*. San Francisco: Harper and Row, 1989.

Hiebert, Theodore. "The Tower of Babel and the Origin of the World's Cultures." *Journal of Biblical Literature* 126 (2007): 29–58.

Hodge, Caroline Johnson. *If Sons, Then Heirs: A Study of Kinship and Ethnicity in the Letters of Paul*. Oxford: Oxford University Press, 2007.

Irigaray, Luce. "Civil Rights and Responsibilities for the Two Sexes." In *Thinking the Difference: For a Peaceful Revolution*, translated by Karin Montin, 65–88. London: Routledge, 1994.

———. "The Cost of Words." In *Je, Tu, Nous: Toward a Culture of Difference*, translated by Alison Martin, 119–32. London: Routledge, 1993.

———. *In the Beginning She Was*. London: Bloomsbury Academic, 2013.

———. *Speculum of the Other Woman*. Translated by Gillian C. Gill (Ithaca: Cornell University Press, 1985.

———. *To Speak Is Never Neutral*. Translated by Gail Schwab. New York: Routledge, 2002.

Jackson, Timothy P. *The Priority of Love: Christian Charity and Social Justice*. Princeton, NJ: Princeton University Press, 2003.

Johnson, Luke Timothy. *The Acts of the Apostles*. Sacra Pagina 5. Collegeville, MN: Liturgical Press, 1992.

Jones, Robert P. *The End of White Christian America*. New York: Simon and Schuster, 2016.

Kahl, Brigitte. "Acts of the Apostles: Pro(to)-Imperial Script and Hidden Transcript." In *In the Shadow of Empire: Reclaiming the Bible as a History of Faithful Resistance*, edited by Richard A. Horsley, 137–56. Louisville: Westminster John Knox, 2008.

Käsemann, Ernst. "The Disciples of John the Baptist in Ephesus." In *Essays on New Testament Themes*, translated by W. J. Montague, 136–48. London: SCM Press, 1964.

Lampe, Peter. "Theological Wisdom and the 'Word About the Cross': The Rhetorical Scheme in 1 Corinthians 1–4." *Interpretation* 44 (1990): 117–31.

Levinas, Emmanuel. *Totality and Infinity: An Essay on Exteriority.* Translated by Alphonso Lingis. Pittsburgh: Duquesne University Press, 1969.

Levine, Amy Jill. *The Misunderstood Jew: The Church and the Scandal of the Jewish Jesus.* San Francisco: HarperSanFrancisco, 2006.

Liew, Tat-siong Benny. "Acts." In *Global Bible Commentary*, edited by Daniel Patte, 419–28. Nashville: Abingdon Press, 2004.

Lim, Timothy H. "Not in Persuasive Words of Wisdom, but in the Demonstration of the Spirit and Power." *Novum Testamentum* 29 (1987): 137–49.

Litfin, Duane. *St. Paul's Theology of Proclamation.* SNTSMS 79. Cambridge: Cambridge University Press, 1995.

Lorde, Audre. "Uses of the Erotic: The Erotic as Power." In *Sister Outsider: Speeches and Essays*, revised ed., 53–59. New York: Crown, 2007.

Lorde, Audre, and Adrienne Rich. "An Interview with Audre Lorde." *Signs* 4, no. 6 (1981).

Malcolm, Matthew R. *Paul and the Rhetoric of Reversal in 1 Corinthians: The Impact of Paul's Gospel on His Macro-Rhetoric.* SNTSMS 155. Cambridge: Cambridge University Press, 2013.

Malina, Bruce J., and John J. Pilch. *Social-Science Commentary on the Book of Acts.* Minneapolis: Fortress, 2008.

Marion, Jean-Luc. *Prolegomena to Charity.* Translated by Stephen E. Lewis. New York: Fordham University Press, 2002.

Marshall, I. Howard. *The Book of Acts: An Introduction and Commentary.* Tyndale New Testament Commentaries. Grand Rapids: Eerdmans, 1980.

Marshall, Peter. *Enmity in Corinth: Social Conventions in Paul's Relations with the Corinthians.* WUNT II/23. Tübingen: J.C.B. Mohr, 1987.

Martin, Dale B. *The Corinthian Body.* New Haven: Yale University Press, 1995.

Martin, Frances. *Acts.* Volume 5 of *Ancient Christian Commentary on Scripture: New Testament.* Edited by Thomas C. Oden. Downers Grove: InterVarsity, 2006.

Mbiti, John S. *African Religions and Philosophy.* 2nd ed. Portsmouth, NH: Heinemann, 1990.

Metzger, Bruce M. *A Textual Commentary on the Greek New Testament.* 2nd ed. New York: American Bible Society, 1994.

Morrison, Toni. "Unspeakable Things Unspoken: The Afro-American Presence in American Literature." *Michigan Quarterly Review* 5, no. 1 (1990): 1–47.

Munck, Johannes. *The Acts of the Apostles.* Garden City, NY: Doubleday, 1967.

Muñoz, Jose Esteban. *Disidentifications: Queers of Color and the Performance of Politics.* Minneapolis: University of Minnesota Press, 1999.

Neusner, Jacob. *The Rabbinic Traditions about the Pharisees before 70.* Volume 3. Leiden: Brill, 1971.

Penner, Todd, and Caroline Vander Stichele. "Script(ur)ing Gender in Acts: The Past and Present Power of *Imperium*." In *Mapping Gender in Ancient Religious Discourses*, edited by Todd Penner and Caroline Vander Stichele, 231–66. Leiden: Brill, 2007.

Pervo, Richard I. *Acts: A Commentary.* Hermeneia. Minneapolis: Fortress, 2009.

Pickett, Raymond. *The Cross in Corinth: The Social Significance of the Death of Jesus.* JSNTSS 143. Sheffield, UK: Sheffield Academic, 1977.

Pogoloff, Steven M. *Logos and Sophia: The Rhetorical Situation of 1 Corinthians.* SBLDS 134. Atlanta: Scholars Press, 1992.

Regev, Eyal. "The Sadducees, the Pharisees, and the Sacred: Meaning and Ideology in the Halakhic Controversies between the Sadducees and Pharisees." *The Review of Rabbinic Judaism* 9 (2006): 126–40.

Román, David. *Acts of Intervention: Performance, Gay Culture, and AIDS.* Bloomington, IL: Indiana University Press, 1998.

Saussure, Ferdinand de. *Course in General Linguistics.* Edited by Charles Bally, Albert Riedlinger, and Albert Sechehaye. Translated by Roy Harris. Chicago: Open Court, 1983.

Schweizer, Eduard. "Die Bekehrung des Apollos, Ag. 18, 24–26." *Evangelische Theology* 15, no. 6 (1955): 251–53.

Scott, James C. *Domination and the Arts of Resistance: Hidden Transcripts.* New Haven: Yale University Press, 1990.

———. *Weapons of the Weak: Everyday Forms of Peasant Resistance.* New Haven: Yale University Press, 1985.

Skinner, Matthew L. *Intrusive God, Disruptive Gospel: Encountering the Divine in the Book of Acts.* Grand Rapids: Brazos, 2015.

Stoellger, Philipp. "The Word of the Cross in the Conflict of Interpretive Power: On the Genealogy of Theology Deriving from the Spirit of Pauline Rhetoric." In *The Wisdom and Foolishness of God: First Corinthians 1–2 in Theological Exploration,* edited by Christophe Chalamet and Hans-Christoph Askani, 201–38. Minneapolis: Fortress Press, 2015.

Strandenaes, Thor. "The Missionary Speeches in the Acts of the Apostles and Their Missiological Implications." *Svensk missionstidskrift* 99 no. 3 (2011): 231–54.

Strawn, Brent A. *The Old Testament Is Dying: A Diagnosis and Recommended Treatment.* Grand Rapids: Baker Academic, 2017.

Tannehill, Robert. *The Narrative Unity of Luke-Acts: A Literary Interpretation.* Minneapolis: Fortress, 1986–1990.

Thistleton, Anthony C. *The First Epistle to the Corinthians.* NIGTC. Grand Rapids: Eerdmans, 2000.

Townes, Emilie M. *Womanist Ethics and the Cultural Production of Evil.* New York: Palgrave Macmillan, 2006.

Trocmé, Etienne. *Le 'Livre des Actes' en l'histoire.* Paris: Presses Universitaires de France, 1957.

Vielhauer, Philipp. "On the 'Paulinism' of Acts." In *Studies in Luke-Acts,* edited by L. E. Keck and J. L. Martyn, 33–50. Mifflintown, PA: Sigler Press, 1980.

Viviano, Benedict T., and Justin Taylor. "Sadducees, Angels, and Resurrection (Acts 23:8–9)." *Journal of Biblical Literature* 11, no. 3 (1992): 496–98.

Weil, Simone. *Waiting for God.* New York: Perennial Classics, 2001.

Welborn, L. L. *Paul, the Fool of Christ: A Study of 1 Corinthians 1–4 in the Comic-Philosophic Tradition.* JSNTSS 293. London: T and T Clark, 2005.

West, Cornell. *Democracy Matters: Winning the Fight against Imperialism.* New York: Penguin, 2004.

White, Adam G. "Not in Lofty Speech or Media: A Reflection on Pentecostal Preaching in Light of 1 Cor 2:1–5." *Journal of Pentecostal Theology* 24, no. 1 (2015): 117–35.

Witherington III, Ben. *The Acts of the Apostles: A Socio-Rhetorical Commentary.* Grand Rapids: Eerdmans, 1998.

Wittgenstein, Ludwig. *Tractatus Logico-Philosophicus.* Translated by B. F. McGuinness and D. F. Pears. London: Routledge, 1961.

Wuellner, Wilhelm H. "Haggadic Homily Genre in 1 Corinthians 1–3." *Journal of Biblical Literature* 89 (1970): 199–204.

Young, Thelathia Nikki. *Black Queer Ethics, Family, and Philosophical Imagination.* New York: Palgrave Macmillan, 2016.

Index

Tower of Babel, 5–7, 11
Townes, Emilie M., 16
trace, 79
Trump, Donald, 16, 22–23

Weil, Simone, 26, 101–102, 109n7
West, Cornell, 22

wisdom, 77–87, 96–98
witness of God, 78–80
Wittgenstein, Ludwig, 77
womanism, 26, 103

Yates, Ashley, 15

About the Authors

Eric D. Barreto, Ph.D., is Weyerhaeuser Associate Professor of New Testament at Princeton Theological Seminary. His publications include *Ethnic Negotiations: The Function of Race and Ethnicity in Acts 16*, *Reading Theologically* (ed.), *Thinking Theologically* (ed.), *Writing Theologically* (ed.), and *"A People for God's Name": Theology and Ethnicity in the Acts of the Apostles* (forthcoming).

Jacob D. Myers, Ph.D., serves as assistant professor of homiletics at Columbia Theological Seminary. His specialties are in homiletics, philosophical theology, and post-structural theory. His publications include *Making Love with Scripture: Why the Bible Doesn't Mean How You Think It Means* (Fortress, 2015) and *Preaching Must Die!: Troubling Homiletical Theology* (Fortress, 2017).

Thelathia "Nikki" Young, Ph.D., serves as assistant professor of women's and gender studies and religion at Bucknell University. She specializes in ethical issues of race, gender, and sexuality and how black queer communities possess, embody, and enact moral excellence. Her first book, *Indecent Family: Black Queers, Ethics, and Imagination*, was published by Palgrave Macmillan in 2016. She is currently working on a second book, tentatively titled *Home Free: A Transnational Ethics of Black Queer Liberation*.

Printed in the USA
CPSIA information can be obtained
at www.ICGtesting.com
LVHW041648121023
760914LV00002B/3